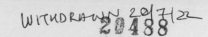

advancing learning. changing lives

Edexcel GCSE

History
Controlled Assessment
CA10 The impact of war on
Britain c.1914–50

Steve Waugh, Victoria Payne and Kirsty Taylor
Series editor: Angela Leonard

A PEARSON COMPANY

Introduction

This unit is about the impact that the First and Second World Wars had on Britain. We will look at how these wars changed the ways in which the government ran the country. Indeed, there were many new laws and government powers introduced to try to make sure both that Britain could keep going and that Britain would win the wars.

The scale of the conflicts meant that more people than ever before were involved directly in fighting the wars and also indirectly in supporting the war effort at home. We will see how the lives of these people were affected and whether any of these changes remained once the wars were won. Finally, we will examine the impact that the First and Second World Wars had on society in general.

Part A of this book covers:

- government organisation for war
- the experience of fighting
- the civilian experience of total war
- the impact of war on society.

For your controlled assessment in this unit, you will learn how to carry out an enquiry (Part A) and how to analyse and evaluate representations of history (Part B). Later sections of this book cover the skills you will need to be successful in unit 4.

Your Part A enquiry will focus in detail on one key question. In Part B you will focus on representations of history: how to analyse, compare and evaluate different views of how civilians responded to the Blitz.

Contents

The impact of war on Britain c.1914–50

Part A Carry out a historical enquiry

A1 Government organisation for war

Learning outcomes

By the end of this topic, you should be able to:

- outline the laws which gave the government extended powers during the First and Second World Wars

- describe and explain the ways in which the government organised the labour force and key industries during the war years

- give examples of government propaganda and the ways in which the government controlled information during the wars

- explain why the government used censorship and propaganda during the wars.

Being at war was not new for Britain – for centuries it had become involved in various conflicts around the world. What was new was the size and scale of the twentieth century conflicts which brought with it a new concept: that of **total war**. This meant that the entire country (including civilians) was involved in the conflict.

Total war: war fought with all available resources, intended to destroy entirely all enemy resistance and affecting civilians as well as soldiers.

Being successful in a total war of this scale meant that many areas of life were going to be affected. There would be many needs that the government would have to address, which can be seen in the diagram below.

Fighting men
More men than ever before were needed to fight on land, sea and in the air.

Military equipment
Uniforms, weapons, transport and other military equipment had to be manufactured to supply the massively increased armed forces.

Essential resources
Raw materials and manufactured goods were required to supply both the armed forces and the civilian population at home, yet many workers were needed to fight.

Needs of Britain in the First and Second World Wars – how could they be achieved?

Controlling information
It was essential to stop information being leaked to the enemy either through the media or through individuals.

Maintaining morale
Keeping people's spirits up so that they continued to support the war and do 'their bit' to help the war effort was important in both conflicts. The support of the civilian population was essential in a time of total war even though thousands of civilians, as well as soldiers, would be killed and injured.

Food
It was quickly realised that there was a real possibility of being starved out of both wars if imports of food did not reach Britain.

Activities

1. Make two tables like the one below – one for the First World War and one for the Second World War.

Britain's war needs	What was needed and why	New government powers	How did the new powers help meet the needs?
Fighting men			
Military equipment			
Essential resources			
Food			
Controlling information			
Maintaining morale			

2. Complete your tables as you read through this section.

Source A: A poster of 1940, featuring Churchill.

New roles and powers

In this section we will look at the role and power of the government and how it was greatly expanded in order to meet the needs of total war.

The government brought in new laws – the Defence of the Realm Act during the First World War (known as DORA) and the Emergency Powers Act during the Second World War. These laws gave the government wide-ranging powers over the lives of British citizens which had never been held by a government before.

This increased level of government control showed that governments were able to make a positive difference to people's lives. This had an effect in peacetime too. After each war, although the role of government reduced, it remained greater than it had been at the beginning of the twentieth century.

Leaders are important during wartime and governments were dominated in both wars by key figures who played major roles.

Lloyd George and Churchill

Lloyd George transformed and greatly expanded the role of government during the First World War. In 1915 he became minister of munitions (see page 10) and then as prime minister, 1916–18, he ensured that government and the country were geared towards total war.

Churchill's role, as prime minister during the Second World War, was different again. He used his skills as a speaker to maintain the morale of the British people, especially after the **Dunkirk** evacuation and during the **Blitz**. As well as his ability to inspire the British people, he was also excellent at picking a good team of government ministers and working with them. For example, he appointed Ernie Bevin as minister of labour, even though they belonged to different parties.

Dunkirk: in May 1940, after the Germans had invaded France, defeated British and French soldiers fled to the port of Dunkirk in Northern France where many were rescued by boat and brought back to Britain.

Blitz: the sustained bombing of Britain by Nazi Germany, 1940–41.

Did you know?

The government even tried to control the amount of alcohol people drank during the wars because of its effects on the workforce!

Results Plus

Watch out

Don't get confused between the two wars. Look carefully at how Britain's needs were handled in each war. What were the similarities and differences?

Government powers 1914–18

People's lives were greatly affected by the passing of the Defence of the Realm Act in 1914. New government powers included the right to take possession of any factory, workshop or piece of land and also to censor newspapers. Here are some of the things people were not allowed to do according to DORA:

talk about military affairs in public places

spread rumours about military affairs

light bonfires or fireworks

buy binoculars

buy whisky or brandy in a railway refreshment room

fly a kite

ring church bells

use invisible ink when writing abroad

melt down gold or silver

trespass on railways or bridges

Activity

3. Working in pairs, choose four regulations from DORA telling people what they could not do. Why do you think the government wanted to control this behaviour?

As the First World War progressed, the government brought in many other measures. These included:

- introducing British Summer Time (putting the clocks forward an hour) to provide more daylight for work in the evening
- controlling the consumption of alcohol, to try to reduce absenteeism from work due to drunkenness – they reduced pub opening hours, gave instructions for beer to be watered down and stopped customers buying rounds of drinks
- appointing special constables to help maintain law and order.

Wider government role 1939–45

In May 1940 (during the Second World War) the Emergency Powers Act was introduced by the government, after the British Army had been forced to retreat from Dunkirk. This was a time of desperation, with France on the verge of defeat and with every likelihood of a German invasion of Britain. The act gave the British government almost unlimited powers over people and property. From then on, civilians could be required to do anything and be sent anywhere.

The government did not just have greater power but also a much wider role in almost every aspect of life, all geared to ensuring victory in the war – as can be seen from Source B.

Source B: An extract from *War and the transformation of British society c.1931–51,* by Steve Waugh and John Wright.

The first half of the war saw the creation of many new ministries: not only a Ministry of Labour but also Economic Warfare, Food, Home Security, Production Shipping, Information and Aircraft Production. By 1943, there were well over 250,000 more civil servants [people working for the government] than before the war. It was soon clear that these ministries, as well as the established ones, had to work by centralised, coordinated, planning. This produced an utterly different way of looking at government from the old approach.

Internment

During both conflicts, the government passed laws which allowed the arrest and imprisonment without trial of people from enemy nations.

Tens of thousands were **interned** during the First World War. The government knew that most of these people (mostly German) posed no threat. However, internment helped to dim the widely held fear of enemy spies living in Britain. Conditions in many internment camps were not good, especially to begin with. At the end of the war many internees were deported, even those who were married to British nationals and who had British children.

Internment of 'enemy aliens' (German, Austrian, Italian and Japanese nationals) also happened in the Second World War. Even those who had fled from Nazi persecution found themselves interned when they arrived in Britain. However, in the Second World War the government and the media did not whip up anti-German feeling to the same extent as during 1914–18. Conditions for those who were interned were better than in the First World War.

Activity

4. Why do you think German people living in Britain during the Second World War were generally treated better than during the First World War?

Organisation of the labour force

First World War

From the early stages of the First World War, British industry began to suffer a desperate shortage of labour. By early 1916, Britain had up to two million fewer workers than were necessary to keep the country going. This was due to the number of men who had volunteered for the armed forces.

The Ministry of Labour was set up to organise the nation's labour force. It introduced the following measures:

- **Reserved occupations** – workers in certain occupations whose skills were needed to keep Britain running (such as miners or farmers) were not allowed to join up and were exempt from **military conscription**.
- **Directed labour** – gave the government the power to force workers to remain in jobs and/or move them to where they were needed.

Despite these measures, as the war continued and more and more men were enlisted in the armed forces, the labour shortage became more acute. Even though many industrialists and the trade unions objected, in March 1915 the Ministry of Labour compiled a register of women who were willing to work and began advertising for women workers. Gradually, more and more women were employed to do 'male' jobs (see page 26).

Second World War

From the start of the Second World War all men aged 18–41 had to register, either to fight or work in a reserved occupation. The Ministry of Labour was revived and could again direct labour.

This time some workers' freedom was severely restricted. Wages and hours of work were strictly controlled, and workers could be moved around. For example, when coal stocks fell dangerously low in 1940, some 30,000 miners had to leave the army and return to their old jobs.

Once again, women were not turned to at first – unemployed men were used to fill the gaps created by those going off to fight but by early 1940 it became obvious that women would again have to be called on. This time from late 1941, unmarried women between 20 and 30 were conscripted to work in industry or the **auxiliary armed services** (see page 15). By 1943 the age range had widened to 19–43. After this time, 90 per cent of single women and 80 per cent of married women were doing work of national importance.

Intern: to force someone to live in a special area or camp.

Military conscription: the system of forcing men and sometimes women to serve in the armed forces.

Auxiliary armed services: these are military services which support the fighting forces but are not directly involved in fighting.

Organisation of key industries

During both conflicts, the government took over industries which it regarded as essential for winning the war and keeping the country going.

Activity

5. Imagine that you work for the Ministry of Labour at a time of total war. Which of the following industries do you think should be protected by the government and why? Explain your choice.
   - coal mining
   - iron and steel works
   - shipbuilding
   - car manufacturing
   - aircraft manufacturing
   - railway network
   - agriculture
   - fisheries
   - textiles and clothing factories.

The First World War: war socialism

Although the Ministry of Labour was set up in the early months of the First World War and some measures were taken to ensure that key workers remained where they were, it was really only the munitions industry which came under total government control from the start of the war (see page 10).

By 1917, however, things were becoming desperate so Lloyd George introduced 'war socialism', which meant that the government took temporary control of most of the resources of the country. (See the diagram below.)

One of the other effects of war socialism was that trade unions became far more important and powerful. Membership doubled, and the government negotiated with union leaders, especially in connection with directed labour and the employment of female workers.

Some features of war socialism in the First World War

Railways
The railway network was taken over so that transport could be coordinated more effectively. In 1914 there had been 120 different railway companies. Lloyd George created a unified system.

Coal
All coal mines were taken over, and production reached an all-time high of 262 million tonnes per year. At the same time, the miners received a national minimum wage, and the safety record improved because of new checks.

Ships
Shipyards were taken over to ensure that enough vessels were built to replace the many being sunk by German U-boats.

Changes to industry during the Second World War

This time, the government was quicker to react. Even before the war had begun in 1939, a new Ministry of Supply was set up which took over the coal, iron and steel industries. Throughout the war, directions in what to produce and which factories to supply were given to each plant in the UK. Not all industries were taken over completely. Instead Ernest Bevin, the minister of labour, worked closely with employers and with the trade unions to make Britain's wartime production as efficient as possible.

Coal supplies remained a problem throughout the war and, from 1942, men were either conscripted or could opt for the mines rather than the armed forces. Those who did were known as the 'Bevin boys'. Men from wealthier backgrounds experienced, for the first time, the often unpleasant working conditions down the mines. Not surprisingly many preferred to join the armed forces.

Agriculture was another area which came under strict government control. Farmers were told what to produce and where to produce it. Many fields were turned from pasture (for animals to graze on) to arable (for growing crops). Men who ran the farms were generally exempt from conscription into the armed forces but this was not the case for the farm labourers. The shortfall in farm labourers was filled partly by prisoners of war but mainly by women from the **Land Army**.

Source C: The front page of a Boy's Own comic from 1944, showing a Bevin boy.

Activities

6. Explain why the coal, iron and steel industries came under total government control in the Second World War.

7. How much do you think this government involvement would have affected workers? Make a list of the positive and negative ways in which workers would have been affected.

Land Army: a British civilian force during the First and Second World Wars made up of women who worked in farming and replaced men who had gone to fight. These women were commonly known as 'Land Girls'.

Did you know?

Nearly 48,000 men were conscripted or volunteered to serve as 'Bevin Boys' during the Second World War. However, it was not until 2007 that their contribution to the war effort was officially recognised when they were awarded a Veterans Badge, similar to those of the armed forces.

ResultsPlus
Top Tip

Students will do well in Part A of their controlled assessment when they show how factors worked together. To explain why the government's role increased, think about the links between: the needs of war, new government powers, people's reactions to new government roles.

Source D: A photograph taken in a munitions factory during the First World War.

Military equipment and munitions

The First World War

In 1915 Lloyd George became Minister of Munitions and described the new government department as having 'no staff, no tables and too many mirrors'. By the end of the war, as a result of his efforts, the ministry was employing a staff of 65,000 and had over three million workers under its direction.

To cope with increased demand, the government set up new munitions factories, which were owned and run by the government. However, these new factories still needed people to work in them and there was an ever-dwindling supply of male labour. It was Lloyd George who insisted on employing women in the government-run munitions factories. This set an example. Previously many employers were willing to employ women to do paperwork, few believed that women were capable of doing manufacturing or engineering jobs. Now the privately run factories began to employ women as well. By 1918, about 60 per cent of all workers in the munitions industry were women (see page 26 for the experiences of these women workers).

The Second World War

Government control over British industry during the Second World War ensured that the armed forces had the equipment necessary for victory. New government-funded factories were opened and production targets were set. Wages and working hours were also set by the government.

In general these targets worked. For example, in 1938 Britain produced 2,000 military aeroplanes; by 1943 it was producing 26,000 each year. There were similar increases in the production of tanks, rifles and machine guns.

The government also recruited more scientists, engineers and inventors to work with the military. They developed and improved technology such as radar to find and destroy enemy aircraft and ships and ciphers to decode secret messages.

Controlling information

From the start of both wars all news, especially bad news, was strictly controlled by the government.

Censorship during the First World War

The Defence of the Realm Act gave the government the powers of **censorship**. Only news issued by army headquarters or the government could be published. Private letters and telegrams were censored. A newspaper could be taken to court if it used unauthorised material.

It was not until November 1916 that the government allowed journalists to be at the war front at all, and their reports had to focus on good news. Newspapers that tried to give more-balanced views of the war, or that were anti-war, such as the *Tribunal*, were closed down.

This censorship aimed to:

- maintain morale and support for the war by ensuring that the public did not find out about the worst features of the Western Front
- make sure that the British people were not exposed to the enemy (German) view of the war (that Germany was in the right as they were fighting a war of self-defence)
- stop sensitive information from leaking out to the enemy as letters or newspaper articles might give away classified military information.

In 1916, the censors examined 38,000 articles, 25,000 photographs and 300,000 private telegrams.

Censorship during the Second World War

The government again had emergency powers that enabled it to control information and ensure the press did not publish and the BBC did not broadcast information that might be helpful to the enemy or might lower morale. Strict guidelines were given about what could (or could not) be published or broadcast. In the first instance, the government preferred to rely on a system of 'self-censorship', whereby publishers and broadcasters censored themselves, but if the rules were breached the penalties could be severe. One newspaper, the *Daily Worker*, was banned in 1941 because it claimed that employers were making money out of the war by exploiting their workers.

The government also used posters to make people aware of accidentally giving information to potential spies. 'Careless talk costs lives' became the motto.

> **Censorship:** the control by a government of the spread of all information that might be useful to the enemy or that might upset the morale of the public.

Activity

8. Imagine you are an army censor. Make a copy of the letter below, written by a soldier on the Western Front. Highlight any words or phrases that need to be removed because they might upset morale or give away military information.

Dear Mam and Dad,
Near Amiens
12 July 1916

I am writing this letter from a trench near Amiens, in France, where the Northumberland Fusiliers are stationed. Yesterday we launched an attack against the Germans. We captured a stretch of their trenches. However, two of my close mates were killed by German machine guns. I've made some really good friends in the trenches. The food is awful and there are rats everywhere. However, we must not give up. It looks like we are getting ready for another attack tomorrow.

Love

Billy

Letters from soldiers at the front to loved ones in Britain were carefully censored. Nevertheless, some servicemen and women devised coded messages to avoid censorship. For instance, the mention of 'yellow' meant North Africa and 'grey' meant Iceland and so on. A letter to a girlfriend suggesting that she painted the ceiling meant that her boyfriend was coming home.

Although censorship severely limited the normal liberties of the British people, there were few complaints during either conflict. The great majority of people accepted it as a necessity of wartime that would end once the enemy was defeated.

Propaganda during the First World War

The government used **propaganda** in the early months of the war to ensure support for the war effort and help persuade young men to volunteer for the armed forces. The British government therefore set about convincing the public that the Germans were evil and had to be stopped. Journalists were encouraged to exaggerate stories wildly to make the enemy appear even worse.

German army bayoneting Belgian babies!

Innocent civilians murdered; women crucified!

Human corpses melted down and made into soap in German factories!

> **Propaganda:** one-sided information used to persuade people to support certain ideas or beliefs.

Propaganda posters were also used to encourage people to go without things and waste less in order to support the war effort. This was especially important in 1917, when German U-boat attacks seriously reduced Britain's food supplies.

Cinema was the newest form of entertainment (see page 26) and the government used it to its advantage. The British Topical Committee for War Films was a group of film companies who got together to make and sell films to the War Department. The committee made the most famous film of the First World War, *The Battle of the Somme*, a propaganda film intended to boost morale and reinforce support for the soldiers at the Front. It was released in August 1916 and was hugely successful, selling 20 million tickets in the first six weeks. The film showed actual scenes from the battle, including real casualties, as well as 'fake' scenes. Many people had their first chance to see what it was really like on the Western Front.

Activity

9. Explain, with examples, two ways in which the British government used propaganda during the First World War.

Source E: A poster used to encourage men to join up in the Great War (another name for the First World War).

Daddy, what did YOU do in the Great War?

Propaganda during the Second World War

Propaganda was also used in Britain during the Second World War to boost morale, maintain support for the war effort and to provide people with information and instructions. However, conscription meant it was not necessary to use it to encourage men to sign up.

Unlike in the First World War, the Ministry of Information (MoI) tried to get across the truth about the horrors of war and avoid giving the public any false hopes of victory. However, its early efforts were seen by the public as dull and uninspiring and government propaganda was most effective when it appealed to British humour (see Source F).

Posters were also used, as they had been in the First World War, to encourage people to conserve food or fuel. In addition, wartime propaganda made good use of the image of the prime minister, Winston Churchill, to inspire support for the war effort and keep up morale. This was particularly important in the months after the Dunkirk evacuation (see page 5) and the defeat of France.

The BBC played an important role in keeping up morale (see page 32). They were selective in what they broadcast on the radio (television was suspended during the Second World War). For example, their propaganda broadcasts on the radio did much to transform the military disaster at Dunkirk into a morale-boosting triumph by mentioning the bravery of the rescue operation and ignoring the humiliation of defeat and retreat.

Source F: A widely published government propaganda poster from 1941.

A2 The experience of fighting

Learning outcomes

By the end of this topic, you should be able to:

- explain how and why the government encouraged people to volunteer in the First World War
- describe the conscription and exemption laws in both conflicts and explain why the government took these steps
- outline how conscientious objectors were treated in both wars
- describe the training experiences of those on the Home Front in both wars
- explain the reasons for and the effects of bombing raids on Britain during the First and Second World Wars.

Volunteering

On the outbreak of war in 1914, Britain's army was quite small at fewer than 250,000 men. In comparison, the German army was nearly four times as large! The British government realised that it needed more men but was reluctant to force men to join the armed forces.

The minister of war, Lord Kitchener, began a massive recruitment campaign to encourage men to join up. Government ministers made speeches around the country, recruitment offices were set up in every town and the general public were bombarded with posters and leaflets.

Another initiative which was successful in terms of increasing the number of volunteers in the early years was the setting up of 'Pals Battalions' (see page 25). The idea was that men would be more likely to serve if they knew that they would be with people they already knew from their local area. Peer pressure and community spirit saw this succeed to such an extent that many towns 'competed' to see who could get the most volunteers and be seen as the most patriotic.

The government recruitment campaign for the first two years of the First World War was very successful. In the first month, half a million men signed up. By 1916, 2.5 million men had volunteered.

Source A: First World War recruits having their medical checks.

Activities

1. List all the reasons you can think of why men would have volunteered for the armed forces between 1914 and 1916. Which do you think would have been the most common reason?

2. Suggest three reasons why some men did not volunteer.

Women volunteers in the First World War

During the First World War, women were recruited into the armed forces for the first time. At first, in 1916, they were used as volunteers in Voluntary Aid Detachments (VADs), where they worked behind the lines as nurses.

However from 1917 to 1918, women were recruited as full-time members of the armed forces:

WAAC

The Women's Auxiliary Army Corps (WAAC) was set up in January 1917. It took over many of the office jobs in the army, which freed the men to fight.

WRNS

The Women's Royal Naval Service (WRNS) was set up in 1917. Women did not go to sea or fight. As with the army, they took over office duties.

WRAF

The Women's Royal Air Force (WRAF) was set up in 1918. Women did not fly the planes or fight. Instead, they carried out routine office duties.

Did you know?

Although women were not allowed to serve as soldiers, one woman did! In 1915, Dorothy Lawrence disguised herself as a man and served for ten days on the Western Front before being discovered.

Second World War 'Home Front' volunteers

Although conscription was brought in for both men and women during the Second World War (see page 16), many people were either too young or too old to be conscripted into the armed forces or were in a reserved occupation.

By May 1940 it was obvious that the Allies were in deep trouble as the Netherlands, Belgium and then France surrendered in quick succession to Germany. An invasion of Britain suddenly became a very real possibility and Anthony Eden, the war minister, asked for male volunteers aged 16–65 years for a Local Defence Force to defend Britain against invasion.

By August around one million men had volunteered for what was now called the Home Guard.

Conscription

Conscription in the First World War

Conscription (see page 7) became necessary because the number of volunteers began to slow down during the course of 1915 due to news of the conditions at the war front and the high numbers of casualties, which were published in local newspapers. Britain was unable to cover the heavy losses incurred, especially on the Western Front.

> **August 1915:** national registration of all single men introduced. This was later extended to married men. The government now had a list of men who could be called upon to fight if necessary.
>
> **January 1916:** the Military Service Act meant all unmarried men aged 18–41 had to serve in the armed forces.
>
> **May 1916:** the act was extended to include married men.

In the years 1916–1918, 3.5 million men were conscripted into the armed forces. There were only four exceptions:

- men in reserved occupations (see page 7)
- men with ill health
- men with family responsibilities (i.e. where someone else in the family would suffer if they were conscripted)
- conscientious objectors (see page 16).

ResultsPlus
Top Tip

In your enquiry, you will get credit for linking bits of information together from different sections. For example, the experience of fighting can be linked to the impact of war on society because men who volunteered or later were conscripted into the army had a medical check-up to see if they were healthy enough to fight. In the First World War people were shocked by the numbers who were not healthy and this led to some improvements in medical services once the war was over.

Conscription in the Second World War

Military conscription was introduced in April 1939 – before the war had even begun – to avoid the mistakes of the First World War. This was the first time conscription had been introduced in peacetime. At first, men were only supposed to serve for six months after they were called up, but most were kept on for the remainder of the war. Between May 1939 and the autumn of 1941, all men aged between 18 and 52 (unless they were conscientious objectors, deemed to be unfit or were working in a reserved occupation) could be conscripted. Unlike the First World War, during the Second World War there were few complaints about conscription. However, there was some criticism of the government for the slow pace with which it was brought in.

By the end of 1940, 200,000 had deferred their call-up for the armed forces because of the importance of their occupation. Over 1 million volunteered or asked for their call-up to be speeded up in the same period.

As well as few complaints, there were two further differences from the First World War:

- From the start of the Second World War all men aged 18–41 had to register – either to fight or work in a reserved occupation.
- In December 1941 the conscription of women was introduced.

Women in the armed forces during the Second World War

After the conscription of women was introduced in 1941 (see page 7) women had to register for work and could choose to join the auxiliary armed services.

The women's armed services included the WRNS, the WAAF and the ATS (Auxiliary Territorial Service). The WRNS was the most popular service followed by the WAAF. By 1944 there were 450,000 women in these services, with 212,000 in the ATS. As during the First World War, the women did the routine office, driving and domestic duties and freed the men to do combat duty.

Despite not being involved in combat, women did hard and often dangerous jobs too. They worked as mechanics, welders, non-combatant pilots, and carpenters. They even worked on anti-aircraft guns – though they were not allowed to fire them. A total of 335 women were killed in the ATS and another 300 wounded.

Activity

3. What differences and similarities were there between recruitment and conscription in the two World Wars?

Conscientious objectors

The law which introduced conscription in 1916 included a clause which stated that those who objected to serving in the armed forces on 'grounds of conscience' could be excused from joining up. A similar clause was used in 1939.

This meant that in both conflicts, men (and women in the Second World War after 1941) who refused to be conscripted because of their religious beliefs or moral objections to the war had to attend a tribunal to prove that they deserved to be exempt from conscription. The tribunal board had three options to choose from for the conscientious objector:

- Total exemption could be granted and objectors would not have to fight or do any work connected with the war effort.
- Partial exemption could be granted which meant they did not have to fight but had to serve in another way, either in the armed forces or at home.
- Exemption could be denied. If objectors still refused to serve then they could be sent to prison.

Source B is an overview of what happened to conscientious objectors in both conflicts.

Source B: Numbers of conscientious objectors in the First and Second World Wars. (Figures are approximate.)

	First World War	Second World War
Claimed exemption on grounds of conscience	16,000	59,000
Granted total exemption	400	3,000
Granted partial exemption	9,500	44,000
Not granted exemption	6,200	12,000
Imprisoned	6,200	5,000

Attitudes to conscientious objectors in the First World War

Although the public generally supported the war, there were significant groups who objected to it such as socialists, and religious groups, for example the Society of Friends (Quakers). Men who were not wearing uniforms, and therefore assumed not to have signed up, were publically jeered and given white feathers as a sign of cowardice.

After conscription was introduced, conscientious objectors aroused much resentment and hostility. They were seen as lazy, shirkers, cowards and even traitors. The general public and politicians seem to have been fairly united in their attitudes as Sources D, E and F reveal.

Source C: A photograph of conscientious objectors at a prison camp.

CONSCIENTIOUS OBJECTORS

The tribunals were run by the military and objectors who were sent to prison often received harsh and brutal treatment. For example, at a Home Office Works Centre in Dyce, near Aberdeen, where tents were the only form of accommodation, many caught pneumonia and several died. At another centre, the prisoners' job was to handle the rotting corpses of animals. In total, 10 conscientious objectors died in prison, 63 died soon after release and 31 suffered breakdowns because of their experiences.

Source D: Written after the First World War by a Quaker, a member of a religious group who believe in non-violence.

> It was right at the beginning that I learnt that the only people from whom I could expect sympathy were soldiers and not civilians. I was waiting in the guardroom when five soldiers under arrest came in. When they asked me what I was in for, I was as simple as possible: 'I am a Quaker and I refused to join the army because I think that war is murder.' 'Murder,' one of them whispered. 'It's bloody murder.' As they went away they each came up to me and shook me by the hand – 'Stick to it matey,' they said, one after the other.

Source E: Comments made by members of the military tribunals judging conscientious objectors in the First World War.

> 'It is such people as you who cause wars…'
> 'You are only fit to be on the end of a German bayonet.'

Source F: From an interview with a man who had been imprisoned for conscientious objection during the First World War.

> Our ankles were tied together and our arms were tied tightly at the wrists to the cross and we had to remain in that position for two hours. The second evening we were placed with our faces to the barbed wire fence. I found myself drawn so closely to the fence that when I wished to turn my head I did so very carefully to avoid my face being torn. To make matters worse, it came onto rain and a bitterly cold wind blew across the top of the hill. Another man, Jack Gray, was put into a sack, thrown into a pond eight times and pulled by a rope around his body.

After the war, when conscientious objectors returned home, hostility against them continued. Many found it impossible to find employers willing to take them on and some were physically attacked.

1939: a more lenient attitude?

The small percentage of conscientious objectors who went to prison during the Second World War highlights that the attitude of the authorities had changed. The tribunals were not allowed to be judged by people in the military and had to include people from all social classes. Politicians even spoke out about the need to respect the views of conscientious objectors.

Source G: Prime Minister Neville Chamberlain in 1939.

> Where scruples are conscientiously held we desire that they should be respected and that there should be no persecution of those who hold them.

Those who were sent to prison were not treated as harshly as during the First World War.

However, the general public did not seem to share this change in attitude. As in the First World War, conscientious objectors were again portrayed as cowards and traitors in the media. They were jeered at in public, some were sacked from their jobs and some were assaulted.

Activities

4. Working in a group, put together arguments for and against conscientious objectors that people at the time would make. Would there be differences between the two wars?

5. Why do you think more people claimed exemption from conscription in the Second World War than the first?

6. 'It took greater courage to be a conscientious objector rather than to join up.' Discuss.

Training

Those who volunteered or had been conscripted into the armed forces in both conflicts went straight into military training. People on the Home Front also needed training for their new roles, whether working in a factory, in the Land Army or in the Second World War in the Home Guard.

On-the-job training

Women volunteers in both conflicts often found themselves in totally unfamiliar situations. For example, many of the Land Army girls were from inner cities and had had no contact with farms or farm animals at all!

Before 1914, married women were not expected to work at all and single women who did have jobs usually worked in domestic service, as nurses or teachers (of girls only). During the First World War, and even more so in the Second World War, women found themselves working as bus or ambulance drivers, as clerks or secretaries, delivering post or milk and working in factories. In most cases women were thrown in at the deep end. They had to learn while they worked and they had to learn fast.

However, it wasn't just women in paid employment who found themselves with new jobs to learn. Both men and women found themselves in other voluntary positions as well as their usual jobs. For example, women volunteered to help those made homeless by bombing while many men in the towns and cities became air-raid wardens or firemen. There were also those on the Home Front who were trained to fight, even though they were not part of the regular army.

The Home Guard 1940–1944

Training of the Local Defence Force began almost immediately after volunteers had signed up in the Second World War. Headquarters of battalions were set up in towns, and companies met locally to train in parish and village halls, factories, offices, pubs, scout huts and people's homes as well as the local countryside.

To begin with there was a serious lack of equipment. Local people donated whatever weapons they had but there still were not enough guns for all the men (see case study on page 20). Nevertheless, the Home Guard battalions began training in earnest, learning how to march, salute, rifle drill, put on and take off **gas masks** and what to do if the Germans invaded.

> **Gas masks:** everyone in Britain was given a gas mask which allowed them to breathe if gas bombs were dropped – but no attacks took place.

Training times varied though most trained every Sunday and a couple of evenings during the week. Training was provided by people with experience within the battalion and also from 'experts' in the regular army. Many of the older men had fought in the First World War and others in the Spanish Civil War. They brought this valuable experience with them and helped train the younger recruits.

As in the regular army, some men were trained for specific things such as bomb disposal, firing anti-aircraft guns or signalling. As the war continued equipment improved.

Home Guard training and duties also depended on which part of the country the battalion was situated in.

- Those near the east or south coast needed to be prepared for an invasion by sea so they patrolled the coast, mostly at night.
- Those inland in rural areas were on patrol for parachute invasions.
- Those in cities where there were air raids often manned anti-aircraft rockets and guns.
- All were prepared for how to sabotage and disrupt an invading enemy as far as possible.

Although the threat of invasion was over by the end of 1943, the Home Guard did not stand down until November 1944. By that time, many Home Guard members had won medals for bravery, 1,206 had been killed and over 500 seriously injured.

Activity

7. 'The Home Guard would not have put up much of a fight if Germany had invaded.'
   Write reasons for and against this statement.

Source H: A Home Guard platoon training how to use explosives to destroy tanks.

Case study: No. 5 'B' company of the 32nd (Aldridge) Battalion South Staffordshire Home Guard

Key events 1940–1941	Comments from Captain H.M. Myers, a member of the platoon
May 1940: Many men volunteer **June 1940:** First meeting in the village hall: 140 members, Commander and NCOs selected. **Training:** Began straightaway every evening after work and on Sundays. **Basic training:** learning to march, load, sight and care for rifles, ring the bells in the local churches, field work and sentry duties. Emphasis on getting to know every inch of local area. **Equipment:** six rifles; no uniforms.	'A very willing bunch of all ages from sixty to fifteen, from all walks of life, and in all sorts of civilian clothes…A mere handful with military experience…' 'All are keen and most willing to learn but we all, including the instructors, make many mistakes…We make the most of every available minute…' 'We sadly lack equipment. Six P14 rifles for a company 140 strong, and those have to be fetched from and returned to the Police Station, three miles away…We acquire .303 dummies and clips by private means…' 'This active work is a splendid antidote to sickening thoughts – Germany, Italy and perhaps Japan against Britain alone!'
July 1940: Night patrols begin, each made up of six men with one NCO. Every man on patrol one night in six. Prepare for enemy invasion – street signs and directions painted over, road blocks set up, etc. **Training:** Reduced to three evenings per week. Focus on ambush training and disrupting an invading army. **Equipment:** 140 rifles, 60 rounds; 140 bayonets. No uniforms.	'we receive a telephone call from Battalion HQ at 23.15 hours on 5 July saying that reliable reports show that an attack is imminent.' 'The rifles have arrived, one per man plus bayonets and 60 rounds per rifle. (God bless America!)' 'The guard report book tells of…long night watches, frequently without sleep…It does not report, however, the full day's work done yesterday or the full day's work which will commence when the guard is dismissed…'
August 1940: **Equipment:** Uniforms and boots arrive for every man. **Training:** Handling plastic explosives, bombs, mortar and land mines, field craft including camouflage, taking cover, how to destroy tanks and more.	'The weeks fly by. We have now been in three months. Good progress is being made in training and everybody is now a little more confident of his ability as a soldier…' 'We are…very proud of our unit and a healthy spirit of comradeship…prevails throughout the platoon.'
Autumn 1940: Nightly air raids in the area and many reports of parachutes falling, which the platoon investigates.	'Sometimes the whole area is ringed with burning and the men experience a feeling of utter impotence when wondering how their wives and families are faring.
Winter 1940–41: Deep snow but night patrols continue. **Equipment:** Battledress and great coats arrived.	
Spring 1941–43: Night patrols reduced to 1 in 15 nights by 1943; night and day exercises and competitions with other platoons; more equipment including different kinds of bomb arrives.	
May 1943: 100 men transferred to work on anti-aircraft defences – platoon disbanded.	

only 13,000 feet. There were 51 Zeppelin raids between 1915 and 1916. Their main target was London, where strict blackout regulations and other precautions were enforced.

The British public soon became angry because of the apparent lack of defence against the Zeppelins. However, the Zeppelin attacks stopped in 1917 due to improved British defences, including the use of searchlights, which meant that the Zeppelins could be easily spotted. Moreover, if a Zeppelin was hit, it burst into flames. The crew had little chance of surviving. In all, Zeppelin raids on Britain killed 564 civilians and injured a further 1,370 people.

German bombing raids, 1916–17

In May 1917 the Germans began to use aircraft known as Gotha IV bombers. These raids had a dramatic effect on British civilians, who had not experienced anything like this before. There were few ways that people could protect themselves since there were no shelters and little warning. For example, in June 1917, a fleet of Gothas carried out a bombing raid on London and part of the east coast in which 162 civilians were killed and 432 injured. Large numbers of civilians began to shelter in underground stations. In total, 850 people were killed in Gotha raids.

Source I: A memorial to the 18 children who were killed in the Gotha raid on Upper North Street School in Poplar, East London, 13 June 1917.

Follow up your enquiry

Research into a Home Guard company or battalion in your area. How similar or different were they to the case study here? Find out:

- What kinds of men made up the company?
- What were their main duties?
- What training and equipment did they have?

Naval and air raids

The First World War was the first conflict for hundreds of years which saw the possibility of civilians being killed in Britain

Naval raids

It was the town of Yarmouth which saw the first attack of the First World War on British soil on 3 November 1914. It was unsuccessful as German ships were driven away by the Royal Navy before they could get close enough. However, the signs were ominous.

The Yorkshire coast towns of Scarborough, Whitby and Hartlepool were raided on 15–16 December 1914 and saw the first civilian casualties of the war – 119 people were killed and many buildings destroyed. There was widespread panic as people fled their homes in search of safety.

The Germans' intentions in attacking these cities were to destroy harbours and military bases, reduce the threat of the much larger Royal Navy and to try to lure the Royal Navy into German waters where the German Navy would stand a better chance of defeating them. They were not successful, partly because of the inaccuracy of bombing from ships.

Attacks by German ships and submarines did continue throughout the war. For example, Scarborough was attacked again in 1917, but the main bombing threats came from the skies.

Zeppelin attacks

From January 1915, Zeppelins began to make bombing raids on British cities. Zeppelins were airships filled with hydrogen and could fly at 4,600 metres (15,000 feet) – well above British fighter planes, which could fly at a maximum height of

The public outcry against these raids forced the government to bring into operation better searchlights, balloons and anti-aircraft guns. As a result, 6 out of 38 Gotha bombers were shot down in a raid on 19 May 1918. The Germans could not afford such losses and called off further raids.

Source J: Rose Moorhouse was six years old and a pupil at the Upper Street North School (see Source I). She was found, severely injured, in the rubble three days after a Gotha bomb hit the school in June 1917.

> We didn't hear anything, no noise, no bomb falling. Next thing I remember was that I felt heavy, I could scarcely breathe. I kept falling into unconsciousness, then waking up, to hear the sound of myself moaning. I couldn't speak and I couldn't move. I had bits of debris in my mouth. Things come into your mind. All I wanted was my mum.

Activity

8. Write a diary entry from the point of view of a person witnessing a bombing raid for the first time.

The Blitz 1940–1941

During the Second World War the German bombing raids were far more serious than in the First World War because advances in technology meant that more powerful bombers and more destructive bombs could be used. These attacks were known as the Blitz, which is a shortened version of the German word *Blitzkrieg*, which means lightning war. The German raids, which began on 7 September 1940, targeted British towns and cities with the aim of destroying civilian morale, forcing the British into submission and undermining British armaments production.

British towns and cities suffered heavy bombing from the autumn of 1940 to May 1941, with the targets usually being military or industrial centres. From May 1941, the attacks became less and less frequent as Hitler diverted resources to the invasion of the Soviet Union.

Some of the British cities bombed during The Blitz in the Second World War.

The town of Clydebank near Glasgow was hit hard in the spring of 1941 due to the importance of its shipyards. Out of 12,000 houses only seven remained undamaged.

Belfast suffered badly in April and May 1941. At least 1,000 people were killed and 150,000 were made homeless.

Liverpool suffered badly with over 4,000 people dying – the highest outside of London. It suffered its worst raid – from over 500 bombers – in May 1941.

Manchester was badly attacked in December 1940.

The naval base at Portsmouth was the target for a massive attack on 10 January 1940 where 930 civilians were killed and 3,000 injured.

Hull was regularly hit between May 1941 and July 1943. Because of the importance of Hull's industry, little was reported of the damage in the media. Around 60% of the population were made homeless as 95% of houses were damaged or destroyed.

Coventry was badly hit by a series of raids in November 1940 with the Germans using incendiary bombs to increase the damage caused. People were so terrified that they fled from the city each night, sleeping with relatives or in open fields nearby.

London was the primary target, especially the docks and factories of the East End. Between 7 September and 2 November 1940, London was bombed every single night, and in one month – December 1940 –12,500 people died.

V1 and V2 raids

There were further air attacks in 1944–45 from V1 and V2 missiles. About 6,000 V1 bombs reached targets in Britain, causing 20,000 casualties and great damage to houses. The V1 was a flying bomb powered by a rocket engine and was nicknamed the doodlebug because of the noise it made. It flew towards the target area and then came down wherever it ran out of fuel. People on the ground could hear the engine cut out and then a shriek as the bomb hurtled to the ground.

The V2 was a more serious threat because it flew at supersonic speed, and could not be seen or shot down until it was too late. It was the first guided missile. About 500 V2s hit London between September 1944 and March 1945 causing over 9,000 casualties.

Did you know?

In his diary, Churchill wrote that the V2s caused people to feel more suspense and strain than during the bombing of 1940–41 because 'The blind, impersonal nature of the missile made the individual on the ground feel helpless. There was little that he could do, no human enemy that he could see shot down.'

Effects on industry

Bombing of industrial targets was generally not effective. Some factories were isolated, unlike housing areas, and they could easily be missed at night. Most factories were able to resume production within two to three days of being hit.

Effects on civilians

In contrast with the effects on industrial production, the effects on civilians were profound. Estimates vary but over 60,000 people were killed by bombing raids, hundreds of thousands were injured and millions were left homeless. Everyday life was seriously affected (see pages 32-33), not to mention the psychological impact of fear and worry.

Activity

9. 'Although fewer in number, the Zeppelin raids of the First World War were more devastating for the British people than the Blitz of 1940–41.' Discuss.

Follow up your enquiry

Find out more about the effect on civilians of attacks by:

- Zeppelins in the first World War
- bombers during the Blitz
- V1 and V2 missiles.

Which place closest to where you live suffered from bombing in the First and/or Second World War? Carry out some research to find out what happened.

Alternatively find out what precautions people took against air raids in your town.

Your conclusion so far

In this topic you have examined the experiences of fighting in Britain during the First and Second World Wars. You have seen how the experience of fighting in total wars affected civilians through:

- volunteering for the armed forces in the First World War and the Home Guard in the Second
- the effects of the introduction and implementation of conscription and what this meant for those who refused to fight on grounds of conscience
- training for their new roles whether in the military or paid or voluntary employment
- the effects of bombing raids.

From what you have learned so far, how much effect did the experience of fighting have on the lives of civilians during the First and Second World Wars?

To answer this question draw two lines across a sheet of paper, one for the First World War and one for the Second World War. Label the ends of the lines 'large effect' and 'little effect'. Decide where on the lines to place the following according to how much you think they affected the lives of British civilians:

- volunteering
- conscription
- naval and air raids.

You can add any other headings you choose.

Then explain in what ways and how much the wars affected the lives of civilians. Be careful to be specific about each war.

A3 The civilian experience of total war

Learning outcomes

By the end of this topic, you should be able to:

- outline the impact of war on civilians' daily life and routine for civilians during the First World War, including rationing, dealing with death and destruction, and changes to work and employment
- outline the impact of war on civilians' daily life and routine for civilians during the Second World War, including rationing, evacuation, travel restrictions, changes in work and employment, and coping with death, injury and destruction.

Impact on daily life and routine: the First World War

Both the First and Second World Wars were wars on a scale which had never been seen before. As 'total wars' the whole of Britain with all its resources was engaged in the conflicts. However, the impact on civilians in the First World War was less far reaching than in the Second World War except for two important areas: **rationing** and dealing with death and injury.

> **Rationing:** the setting of a fixed allowance of food and other provisions for each person to prevent shortages.

Rationing

A key role of government and one of the aims of DORA (see page 5) was to control food supplies to prevent Britain from being starved out of the war. By 1917 the Germans were using their submarines to stop supply ships from getting through to Britain from America and the continent. In April 1917 Britain had only six weeks' worth of wheat stores left. Food was so scarce that prices rose sharply and queues to buy food grew. Coal was also in short supply and, from October 1917, it was rationed.

The government was, at first, reluctant to bring in compulsory food rationing. Instead, it asked people to limit themselves voluntarily each week to:

Two and a half pounds of meat

Three-quarters of a pound of sugar

Four pounds of bread

But voluntary rationing did not work; the food shortages continued and the queues for food grew longer. Moreover, the rich seemed to have access to as much food as they wanted while others went without, and this caused widespread resentment. Therefore, in January 1918, the government introduced compulsory rationing. Everybody was issued with a ration card, and had to register with a local butcher and grocer. Every adult could have the following ration each week:

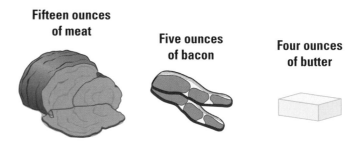

Fifteen ounces of meat

Five ounces of bacon

Four ounces of butter

Rationing worked. Queuing more or less stopped, and the system was seen as fair. Indeed, many poorer people became healthier because they got a better share of healthy food.

Activity

1. Give two reasons for compulsory rationing and two achievements of rationing.

Death on an unimaginable scale

The second area which had an enormous impact on civilians during the First World War was coping with death in the family. There were massive numbers of casualties, especially on the Western Front. By the end of the war over 700,000 men had been killed and twice that number injured. This was a huge shock to a civilian population, which lived in constant fear of a telegram bringing bad news to their door.

Brothers, friends and work colleagues enlisted together in Pals Battalions (see page 14). This meant that, when things went wrong, families and whole towns lost a generation of young men and were swamped with grief.

By 1915, transporting the dead back to Britain for burial had become impractical so the government took the decision that war cemeteries would be set up near the battlefields overseas. This meant that many men were buried in places that would be totally inaccessible to their loved ones.

Once the First World War was over, many war memorials were set up around the country which provided families and friends with somewhere to focus their grief and to commemorate their war dead.

Source A: A national memorial to those soldiers who had died in the First World War – the Cenotaph – is unveiled at a ceremony in 1920. The unknown soldier was buried during this ceremony at Westminster Abbey. Thousands flocked to pay their respects.

Did you know?

One of the best known Pals Battalions is the 11th Battalion East Lancashire Regiment – the Accrington Pals. On the first day of the Battle of the Somme (1 July 1916) the entire battalion was virtually wiped out: of 720 men, 584 were killed, wounded or missing. The devastation felt in Accrington can only be imagined.

Follow up your enquiry

Visit your local First World War memorial. How many soldiers from your area died? Find out what the town population was during each war and compare the figures.

Caring for the injured

It became obvious fairly early on in the First World War that existing hospitals in Britain would not be able to cope with the huge numbers of casualties returning from the front as well as the needs of the civilian population. Some existing hospitals were converted into military ones. Other new permanent hospitals were built but more frequently other buildings were used as hospitals for the duration of the war. Country houses were especially popular as they were usually out of the view of the public and allowed the wounded to recover in peace.

KEEP MOVING

Work and employment

Some people's working lives were hugely affected by the First World War. Men in industries which were important for the war effort, such as coal mining, were exempt from recruitment or conscription (see page 7). That did not mean that their working lives were not affected. In fact men in reserved occupations felt government intervention on an unprecedented scale:

- In many industries, targets were set for the types and numbers of product produced.
- For some, there were wage restrictions.
- Strikes and lock-outs were banned.
- Working hours generally increased: 10-hour days became the norm. Time off was rare and some national holidays were cancelled.
- Skilled workers had to stay or move to where they were needed – they could not choose.

Women enter the workforce

Although women did work before the First World War, they worked mainly in jobs such as nursing, teaching, the textile industry and domestic service. Employment in engineering and manufacturing therefore brought huge changes to the lives of those women who were employed in these areas.

For example, female munitions workers (see page 10) worked very hard, doing 12-hour shifts, seven days a week, but they earned good money compared with what they were used to. A female munitions worker's average wage was more than double that of the average wage for domestic service. The work was also dangerous. Sometimes they developed lead poisoning, or illnesses from the chemicals, which caused their hair to fall out and turned their skin yellow. This earned these women the nickname 'canaries'. Some workers were even killed. In 1917 a fire in Silvertown munitions works in East London caused an explosion that killed 69 people and injured 400.

Other women became part of the Land Army and were sent to help out on farms all over the country. However, the number of women who did these 'manual' jobs was fairly small and most were forced to give them up once the war was over. A far greater impact was on office jobs, where women were employed for the first time in large numbers and were more likely to be able to continue once the war was over.

Generally, the number of working women was still fairly small and the changes applied only to some single women. Married women were generally unaffected.

ResultsPlus
Watch out

Many students make the mistake of saying that 'all women's lives were changed hugely by the First World War as they started working for the first time'. It varied depending on many things, such as location. Although it is true that, by the end of the war, more women were employed than before and some jobs traditionally thought of as 'men's work' were opened up to women, numbers were still quite small and for many women employment did not change at all.

Coping day-to-day

The government realised that entertainment would need to play a significant role in maintaining morale and providing escapism from the horrors of the First World War.

Film

People read newspapers both for amusement and for information about what was happening at the Front. However, in 1914, the newest means of informing and influencing the masses was the cinema. By 1917, there were 4,500 cinemas in Britain. The largest percentage of cinema audiences was made up of young wage earners – especially females – who wanted to get away from thoughts of absent loved ones. Hollywood movies were shown because they generally provided glamour, romance and an escape from the realities of war. People also flocked to see the propaganda war films made by the British Topical Committee for War Films (see page 12).

Activity

2. Create a table or diagram which summarises all the ways in which day-to-day lives were affected by the First World War.

Impact on daily life and routine: the Second World War

Generally, the impact on daily life and routine during the Second World War was far greater and affected the overwhelming majority of the population in one way or another. This was mainly because of the greater threat from bombing raids and the very real threat of German invasion.

Rationing

As in the First World War, the government was aware that there was a very real risk of Britain being 'starved out' of the war. It therefore introduced compulsory rationing much more quickly. In January 1940 the Ministry of Food under Lord Woolton worked out fair food rations. At first only butter, sugar and bacon were rationed. Eventually, almost all food except seasonal fruit and vegetables was rationed (see Source B).

Rationing soon went beyond food. Almost every other essential article could be bought only with coupons. In other words, even if you were rich, you could not legally get extra rations because you had the same number of coupons as everyone else. Even the royal family had ration books. Rationing was a success although there were some shortcomings.

Source B: The weekly ration for an adult

Meat	1–2 shillings-worth and a pennyworth
Bacon	4oz to 8oz
Cheese	1oz to 8oz
Fat	1oz to 8oz
Eggs	1 to 2
Tea	2oz to 4oz
Sugar	8oz to 16oz and 2lb for jam making
Sweets and chocolate	3oz to 4oz
Dried milk	1 tin
Dried eggs	one-eighth of a packet

The government also used other measures to control food supplies:

- The 'Dig for Victory' campaign encouraged people to grow vegetables and keep chickens and pigs. Private gardens were turned into vegetable patches. Playing fields and railway embankments were ploughed up.
- There were campaigns to avoid waste. For example, boy scouts and girl guides collected scraps for pigs.

Activity

3. In what ways was food rationing better organised during the Second World War than the First?

Achievements of rationing

Achievements	Limitations
✓ It was a fair system that ensured that the poorer people were adequately fed with generally healthy food.	✗ The rich could buy extra rations on the black market.
✓ It helped to unite people as they were all, rich and poor, sharing the same rations.	✗ Very large families with several ration books were better off than small families with one or no children.
✓ The quality of rationed clothes was guaranteed by the government's utility mark.	✗ Food supplies were more plentiful in certain areas, for example, vegetables in rural areas and pork and bacon were not rationed in Northern Ireland.

Evacuation

Evacuation was brought in just after the German invasion of Poland, in September 1939, due to the fear of air attack. About 1.5 million people were evacuated from towns or cities to live with families in the 'safer' countryside.

Reasons for evacuation

The British government believed that the Germans would bomb British towns and cities in order to destroy the morale of the people and force Britain to surrender. Therefore evacuation measures were put in place to protect civilians from bombing and gas attacks. Children were to be protected by being moved from the likeliest targets, the cities, to the countryside, where it was thought they would be safe.

Source C: A photograph of children being evacuated, September 1939.

The organisation of evacuation

Children of school age, children below school age if accompanied by their mother or another responsible person, pregnant women and blind people were all eligible for evacuation. It was voluntary but the government used many propaganda posters to encourage it.

Many parents were reluctant to be separated from their children but accepted they would be safer in the country. Parents were told what the children needed to take with them and where they were to assemble for evacuation. The evacuation began on 1 September 1939. Many city schools were closed, and teachers went with the children to the countryside to carry on teaching them.

At their destinations the evacuees gathered in village halls or schools, where they were chosen by the foster family they were to live with. However, homesickness and the **phoney war** meant that many children had drifted back to the cities by Christmas 1939.

When German bombers began blitzing London in 1940, a second evacuation from the cities took place. There was a further wave of evacuations in 1944 when the Germans used their V1 flying bombs and V2 missiles to bomb Britain.

Evacuation: the process of moving people from towns and cities into the countryside for safety, to protect them from German bombing.

Phoney War: the period from September 1939 to April 1940 when little fighting took place and there were no enemy bombing raids.

Activities

4. Either:

   a. Imagine you are a parent – write a letter to your homesick child explaining why he or she has to be sent away.

   Or:

   b. Design a poster or write a radio broadcast persuading parents to part with their children.

5. 'Evacuation at the start of the war was unnecessary.' Discuss.

Experiences of evacuation

The children had varied experiences of evacuation, some pleasant and some unpleasant:

- Evacuees were not used to rural life and there was a clash between city and country values.
- It meant that some children, from poor inner city areas, saw the countryside for the first time.
- The organisation was sometimes poor, especially the way in which the evacuees were chosen by their foster parents.
- Evacuees often found themselves in homes where they had to cope with different standards of behaviour.
- Many evacuees stayed with better-off people and were given a better standard of living, for example better food.
- Some evacuees were treated poorly and were not well looked after.
- Evacuation also showed better-off people in the countryside the social problems of families living in inner city areas and increased the demand for change.

Experiences often depended on the motivation of those who took in evacuees. Many foster families genuinely wanted to help while others agreed to it because they wanted the money or wanted extra workers for the home or farm. Some people tried to avoid taking evacuees altogether.

Evacuation had a huge impact on the foster families. Some children did not react well to having 'foster' brothers and sisters thrust upon them. Older couples whose own children had left home suddenly found themselves with children again. Childless couples who had no experience of looking after children were thrown in at the deep end.

Source D: The memories of Rita Wright, written in 1989. She was evacuated at the age of nine from the East End of London.

> One really good thing about being evacuated to the countryside was the fact that my health improved so much. Although my parents had fed me well, I suffered from pneumonia every winter because of the crowded living conditions at home. From the time I was evacuated I never suffered from it again. The abundance of locally produced fruit and vegetables kept me very healthy.

Source E: An interview with the actor Michael Caine, who remembers life as an evacuee.

> The woman said, 'Here's your meal' and gave us a tin of pilchards between the two of us and some bread and water. Now we'd been in a rich woman's house before, so we said: 'Where's the butter?' And we got a sudden wallop round the head. What we later found out was that the woman hated kids and was doing it for the extra money. So the meals were the cheapest you could dish up.

Activities

6. Evacuation had a huge effect on the parents, the foster families and the evacuees themselves. Draw up a table of feelings (both positive and negative) that each might have felt about evacuation.

7. Was evacuation a success? Give reasons for and against before coming to a conclusion.

Follow up your enquiry

Did evacuation affect the area where you live? Were children (or others) evacuated out of your town/city? Did families in your town/village take in evacuees?

Carry out research to find out experiences of evacuation in your area.

Travel

Travel was another area affected by the war. Getting around day-to-day could be very difficult. There were official travel restrictions put in place by the government. These restrictions depended on where you were and where you were trying to get to. People travelling longer distances needed special warrants and had to explain their reasons for the journey before they were granted. The Emergency Powers Act also gave the police the power to stop and search anyone.

It was not just official travel restrictions that prevented people from getting around. The government encouraged people not to travel unless they really needed to (see Source F). For those who did travel, there were other factors to consider which can be seen in the diagram.

Source F: A poster issued by the Railway Executive Committee during the Second World War.

Activity

8. Give reasons why the government wanted to prevent people from travelling around during wartime.

Lack of trains

The railways were under government control and trains were needed to transport troops and supplies for the war. There were still some trains that were run for civilians but these were often overcrowded and late.

Blackout

During the Blitz, travel within the cities was reduced as people were afraid of being hit by the bombs but also because they could not see due to the blackout. Car accidents increased.

Impact on travel

Destruction of transport

Bombing badly affected transport in some areas. Roads and railway lines were destroyed. Travel on the underground was even disrupted as some stations were flooded by burst water pipes.

Rationing

Petrol was increasingly rationed during the Second World War, which meant that car travel was massively reduced anyway.

ResultsPlus
Watch out

Travel is an example which illustrates that people's experiences during the war years could be vastly different. Never generalise by saying things like 'everyone found travelling around much more difficult'. Be specific about which groups of people you are referring to. For example, people in London and major cities found travel more difficult during the Second World War than people in other parts of the country where blackout restrictions were not in place and transport lines had not been destroyed.

Work and employment

For those in reserved occupations in the Second World War, government intervention in their working lives was similar to that in the First World War (see page 26). This time, however, there were a greater number of women workers as, for the first time, women were conscripted (see page 16). This had a huge impact on the lives of these women, many of whom were married. Many entered work for the first time and took on traditional 'men's jobs'. However, when the war ended, many women had to leave their jobs to make way for men.

Voluntary work

Many men's working days did not finish once they left their paid employment. In the Second World War, many joined organisations voluntarily such as the Air Raid Precautions Service, the Fire Brigade, Heavy Rescue Squads or the Ambulance Service. Others joined the Home Guard (see pages 18–20).

Women (including many who were married) also volunteered for various tasks which were not paid, such as the Women's Volunteer Police Service in the First World War and the Women's Voluntary Services in the Second World War. It was also mainly women who bore the brunt of the extra work involved in taking in evacuees (see page 28). Many of these women had homes to run and children of their own to look after as well.

Many people were willing to do these things for nothing as they liked to think they were 'doing their bit' for Britain. It was often exhausting but it could be enjoyable too and frequently brought more freedom, especially for women who met many new people and did new things.

Activity

9. Jot down all the ways in which people's work and employment may have changed during the Second World War. Who would have been unaffected by these changes? Whose lives would have been changed most dramatically?

Coping with death, injury and destruction

After the horrific shock of the number of deaths in the First World War, Britain was perhaps more prepared. Most importantly, the 'experiment' of Pals Battalions, which caused such devastation to communities in 1914–18, was not repeated.

The number of military deaths in the Second World War was less than in the First World War. Again, soldiers were usually buried where they fell and moved to a war cemetery close to the battlefield once the war was over. For those killed in the Far East, this meant a massive distance between grieving families and their loved ones. Memorials sprang up all over the UK, in villages, towns and cities, often next to the First World War memorials.

Military deaths may have been fewer but the second conflict brought death and the fear of death right onto the streets of Britain through bombing raids. People had to cope, not just with the deaths of soldiers but with the deaths of civilians including women, children and the elderly.

Caring for the injured

Medical needs in Britain in the Second World War were also greater than in the first because of the number of civilian casualties. The government set up a national Emergency Medical Service. This brought all hospitals under the control of the Ministry of Health (see page 40). New hospitals (permanent and temporary) were built and new equipment was provided by the state. These hospitals provided free treatment and helped to pave the way for the creation of the NHS once the war was over.

Coping day-to-day

Again the government realised that entertainment would play an important role in keeping up the morale of the British people. The cinema was popular and between 25 million and 30 million cinema seats were sold every week in Britain. The Ministry of Information set up the Crown Film Unit to make official propaganda films, many of which were directed by Humphrey Jennings. It made short, information documentaries such as *Listen to Britain* as well as longer fictional documentary-style films such as *Close Quarters*. All showed heroic actions by British people.

Radio

The most popular form of entertainment was the radio and it became very important for many people. There was a host of programmes featuring British and American singing artists, with the national favourite being *Music While You Work*. In 1941, there were 21 dance programmes a week on the radio – with the most popular being *Victor Sylvester's Dancing Club*.

Humour was an important method of keeping up people's morale, especially humour that poked fun at the Home Front and government rules and regulations. *It's That Man Again* (ITMA) enjoyed a massive following. It starred Tommy Handley, who played the 'Minister at the Ministry of Aggravation and Mysteries'. It enabled radio listeners to poke fun at all the wartime bureaucracy.

BBC radio was a key method of government propaganda during the Second World War. The news bulletins had massive audiences and had a reputation for truth, reporting reverses and victories alike. Nevertheless, it was subject to censorship. For example, reports about weather conditions were not allowed as these might prove useful to the enemy.

Activity

10. 'The cinema played the most important role in maintaining morale during the two world wars.' Discuss.

Dealing with destruction

Unlike the First World War, there was an expectation that civilians would be targeted by bombing raids in the Second Word War. Therefore, local councils started building air-raid shelters as early as 1935. The Air Raids Precautions Service was set up in 1937 and air-raid wardens began volunteering. Information about how to build shelters and what to do to protect houses was distributed in many ways, including on cigarette cards. Despite these precautions, few civilians would have anticipated the extent of the raids.

Activities

11. Study the flow diagram. For each of the services which helped in the immediate aftermath of a raid, write down what kinds of things they would have done.

12. On a scale of 1–10 how well prepared do you think civilians were for the bombing? Explain your answer.

Coping with air raids

Prevention

Barrage balloons put up to stop German planes flying low.

Sandbags put up to try to prevent damage.

Blackout – street lights turned off, windows covered, etc., so targets could not be seen by the bombers.

Individuals tried to protect their homes and businesses – reinforcing windows and doors, keeping possessions safe.

Making sure air-raid shelters were equipped with necessary food, water, blankets, etc.

As planes approached

Air-raid sirens sounded.

Many people took cover in shelters or elsewhere.

Air-raid wardens patrolled with whistles and took people to shelters.

Immediate aftermath

Professional services:

- Fire Brigade
- Heavy Rescue Squads
- Ambulance Service
- Utilities repair parties (for gas, water and electricity supplies).

Voluntary services made up of people like the Air Raid Precautions Service and Women's Voluntary Services:

- rescue parties
- first-aid parties
- Auxiliary Fire Service and Fire Guard
- mobile canteens.

During the Second World War, bombs were dropped on the same towns every night for weeks, sometimes months. Buildings were patched up as well as they could be but little could be done while the raids were happening.

Many of the homeless found shelter with friends or relatives. Others went to 'rest centres' where simple accommodation was provided by the local council. These were usually either churches or schools which were no longer being used because their pupils had been evacuated. They were run by volunteers, often from the Women's Voluntary Services, who also ran clothing exchanges and canteens to help those who had lost everything.

Rest centres provided only a short-term solution until people could find alternative housing. Those who could not afford it were given council flats or houses with minimum furniture. It wasn't until the Blitz ended in May 1941 that any rebuilding began at all. Rebuilding didn't really start properly until the war was over (see pages 42–43).

Your conclusion so far

In this topic you have studied the civilian experience of total war, specifically:

- the reasons for and experiences of evacuation and rationing
- the impact of war on day-to-day travel
- the changes in work and employment, for both men and women
- the ways in which the civilian population coped with death, injury and destruction.

From what you have learned so far, compare the impact of the two world wars on the lives of civilians. To answer this question:

- describe and compare the impact of government initiatives on civilians in both wars
- assess how far employment and work changes impacted on civilians in both conflicts
- compare the impact of military and civilian deaths and destruction caused by bombing raids in the two wars.

Finally decide whether one war had a greater overall impact than the other on civilians.

Source G: A Rescue Party takes a tea break during the Blitz.

A4 The impact of war on society

Learning outcomes

By the end of this topic, you should be able to:

- describe and explain some of the changing social attitudes of this period
- explain the impact of new government powers in wartime
- evaluate the change in the role and status of women during both wars
- outline the improvements in medical services brought about by both wars
- explain whether Britain was really turned into 'a land fit for heroes' after 1918
- describe and explain the changes after the Second World War – post-war reconstruction, housing and welfare.

Changing social attitudes

The experiences of living and working on the Home Front in both world wars did create greater national unity and demand for a more equal society. Indeed, the First World War accelerated the process leading to votes for more men and for some women. However, this desire for a more-equal society was more apparent during the Second World War because of the impact of rationing and evacuation. These changing experiences were not brought about just by the conflicts themselves but by government action.

Greater government role

Both wars saw the government take a much greater role in people's lives, which was generally accepted without complaint by the public. It showed the benefits of greater control by central government. In other words, the war years had proved that governments were able to make a positive difference to people's lives.

Rationing

Rationing was seen by the British public as both necessary and fair. Rich and poor alike were given the same rations. Moreover, many, especially the poor, had never had such a good diet. This encouraged many to insist that this standard of living should be maintained for all people once the conflict ended.

Evacuation

The evacuation of children from poorer inner-city areas to more wealthy homes in the countryside (see page 28) also stimulated demand and support for a more-equal society in the Second World War. Many foster parents realised, for the first time, the poor conditions in which these children normally lived.

These experiences created a genuine desire to produce a new society in which people were protected from the problems of poverty and ill health. The election of a Labour government in 1945 was very much due to this desire for social change.

Source A: Evacuated children in the Second World War having a bath to get rid of lice, fleas and nits. Many people were shocked at the condition of evacuees.

Change in the role and status of women

Changes for women, 1914–1918

Before the First World War women were very much second-class citizens:

- They did not have the vote.
- They had few job opportunities.
- Jobs were generally low paid.
- They were expected to marry, have children and look after the home.

As explained on pages 15 and 26, the First World War saw women playing a crucial role on the Home Front, especially in employment and the women's armed forces. This did much to change some people's attitudes to votes for women, and their employment opportunities.

The First World War brought other changes to women's lives, mainly as a result of the work they did. Women had to adapt to new ways of dressing for the work they were doing – having short hair or wearing trousers, for example. Some women appeared in uniform, in roles ranging from railway porters to ambulance drivers.

Women gained much greater freedom. With fewer men around, chaperones (women who accompanied wealthier girls when they went

out) became less common. Full wage packets meant that women had money to spend. They now smoked, drank in pubs, went to the cinema, on bicycle trips and on shopping trips in town unsupervised. Some older people were scandalised, and troops returning home from France were amazed. However, in other respects, there was little change.

Did the attitudes of men towards women change?

Despite the warm welcome reported in the papers, many women were met with hostility when they began their new jobs in farms, hospitals and factories. This resentment continued for some but many men were amazed at the quality of the work women produced. In some industries women's production rates were better than men's. However, despite some men acknowledging that women were capable of work, most men thought of it as a temporary measure only necessary until the war was over. Most continued to believe that a woman's only place was in the home.

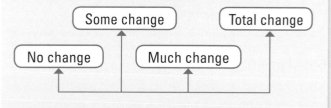

Developments in the position of women, 1918–1939

During the **inter-war** years, women did make some progress. However, there was little or no change in employment opportunities.

Political position

There was some progress in the political position of women. The Representation of the People Act, which was passed in 1918, gave women aged 30 and over the vote. It also gave the vote to the few remaining men over 21 who did not have it. This was due partly to the determination of the government to extend the vote to soldiers who had fought in the war.

However, younger women, in their twenties, were disappointed with the age limit. They were considered too young and immature to cope in a responsible way with a vote. The real reason they were not included was that men feared this would mean a female majority in voters, due to the death of so many men during the First World War.

In 1919 Nancy Astor became the first woman MP to take her seat in Parliament. In 1928, women aged 21 and over were given the vote. At last, they had equal voting rights to men.

> **Flappers:** Young women of the 1920s who challenged traditional ideas through fashion and social habits.
>
> **Inter-war:** between the two world wars.

Social position

There was some progress in women's social position. Labour-saving devices, such as washing machines and fridges, reduced the hours needed on housework and allowed women more leisure time. Better advice about contraception meant that some women could choose when to have children and to have fewer of them.

Moreover, the First World War had given many women greater confidence and had changed their attitude to their appearance and social habits. Young women no longer had chaperones (aunts or older females who accompanied them). They were able to go to the cinema or to dances with boyfriends without being accompanied. Women's clothing became much simpler and less restrictive, and make-up became acceptable. Some women even dared to wear one-piece swimming costumes, instead of the pre-war costumes with sleeves and skirts. **Flappers** were the most extreme example of these social changes. Flappers were young women, in their twenties, who challenged the old ideas about women's fashion. They wore revealing clothes, with short skirts, used a lot of make-up and had short hair. They drank and smoked in public and performed modern dances such as the Charleston.

Progress was also made in women's legal rights. In 1923, they were given the same right as men to seek divorce on grounds of adultery. The Property Act of 1925 allowed married women to hold and dispose of property on the same terms as their husbands.

Employment position

In 1918, 3,000 women were asked: 'Do you wish to return to your former work or stay in the job you are doing now?' Of those women, 2,500 said: 'Stay in the work I'm doing now'. However, as soon as the war ended, women were expected to give up their war work. Women who tried to hold on to their jobs were criticised by men and even, in some cases, physically attacked.

It was argued that women who stayed in these jobs were depriving men of jobs. Women returned to their traditional, unskilled, low-paid jobs or their roles as housewives. By the 1930s women's wages were only half those of men, even if they were doing the same job.

However, there was some progress. The Sex Disqualification Removal Act of 1919 meant that women could no longer be barred from any job because of their sex. In theory, they could now enter the professions, such as the law and architecture. However, the law still applied only to single women. Once married, a woman had to give up her job. In 1925 women were allowed to work for the government in the Civil Service for the first time.

Activities

4. Work in pairs. Make a copy of the following scales.

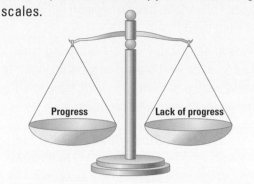

Make a list of progress or lack of progress in politics, social position and employment and place them on the scales. Overall, do you think women made progress in the inter-war years? Explain your answer.

The impact of the Second World War on women

As we have seen, women played an important role on the home front during the Second World War, in industry, the armed forces and various voluntary bodies. This, in turn, influenced attitudes towards women's rights during and after the war although, once again, in many respects there was little lasting change.

Pay

Although there was some improvement, women continued to be paid less than men for doing the same job, especially in factory work, where they usually received about 75 per cent of a man's wage (see Source B).

Source B: Average weekly wages for men and women in July 1943 in pounds, shillings and pence.

	Weekly wage	In today's money*
Men over 21 years	£6 1s 4d	(£6.07)
Men under 21 years	£2 7s 11d	(£2.40)
Women over 18 years	£3 2s 11d	(£3.15)
Women part-time workers	£1 9s 0d	(£1.45)
Women under 18 years	£1 13s 11d	(£1.70)

*Figures do not take into account inflation.

Attitudes of women

Despite all this, many women were pleased to be involved in useful work that helped the war effort. Not all women believed they should be paid the same as men. Others felt that, even if they were not as well paid as the men, they were still earning much more than they were used to getting before the war. Before the war the average woman's wage was about £2 a week. During the war some women doing dangerous munitions work were earning as much as £10 a week.

The war did change the attitudes of some women. War work gave them far more confidence and self-respect. They became far more confident about themselves and their abilities. Many enjoyed the independence and freedom the war had given them.

Source C: Women engineers maintaining a fighter plane for the RAF in 1942.

Attitudes of men

Many men, especially employers and politicians, were impressed with the work done by women.

The trade unions accepted women workers much more readily than they had done in the First World War. The Trades Union Congress (TUC) campaigned to make sure that women were treated the same as men. For example, the TUC successfully complained about the fact that women were paid 25 per cent less and received lower accident compensation than men in the Rolls-Royce armament factories.

Moreover, the government even began to help women with child-care commitments. They provided nurseries and encouraged employers to allow women with children to job share. By 1944 there were 1,450 nurseries, compared to 104 before the war. Most closed when the war was over.

So there was not exactly a revolution in attitudes to women's role in society. The majority of men continued to believe that the traditional roles of women were as wives and mothers, and that once the war ended, they should return to the home.

Source D: An advert for new cookers, 1947.

Activities

5. Give one example of a change and one of the lack of change in pay for women during the Second World War.

6. Work in pairs. Copy out the following table. Compare the part played by women in the two world wars and then fill in your table to show the similarities and differences.

	Similarities in the two wars	Differences in the two wars
Work done by women	In virtually all industries women replaced men who had gone to fight.	Far greater numbers of women doing war work in Second World War.
Women's pay		
Attitudes of men to women's work		

7. Which war brought the greater change in the position of women? Explain your answer.

8. Give two examples of the lack of change in the position of women by 1950.

9. 'The Second World War transformed the lives of women.' Discuss.

Follow up your enquiry

Research your local area. Can you find examples of jobs done by women during the war years? How many women continued to be employed once the war was over?

Did the role of women really change, 1945–1950?

YES

✔ The war had given many women more confidence and self-respect. They had shown that not only could they do the same jobs as men but, in many cases, they could do them better.

✔ More types of employment had been 'opened up' to women – before the First World War, just teaching and nursing were dominated by women. By 1951, these had been joined by two other types of employment where women dominated: clerks and shop workers.

✔ The number of married women in paid work had increased by 1951.

✔ There was some change in attitudes towards married women working. In the 1950s some women did find work when their children were growing up.

ResultsPlus
Top Tip

Those students who do well will give examples of both how the position of women changed and how it stayed the same during this period rather than just showing one side of the argument.

Improvements in medical services

Before the First World War, health provision for people in Britain was a mixture of people paying privately, charity-funded hospitals and some local authority funding. The National Insurance Act of 1911 provided free medical treatment and sick pay to male workers who made payments into a fund, along with their employer and the government. However, this applied only to certain men and didn't cover their families or female workers at all.

NO

✘ Most women willingly left their wartime jobs because they wanted to return to the home. A government survey of 1947 revealed that 58 per cent of women believed that married women should not go out to work. Many had delayed having children during the war and now decided that they wanted to start families.

✘ Women's career opportunities weren't drastically improved by the war. For example, the new opportunities in areas such as metal manufacturing and engineering lasted only as long as the war. The shutting down of nurseries after the war meant the end of jobs for women with children.

✘ They continued to make only slow progress in professions such as medicine and law. As late as 1961 only 15 per cent of doctors and 3 per cent of lawyers were women.

✘ The Equal Pay Commission, set up in 1944, reported in 1946 that the average male manual worker's wage was £5.70 a week, while the wage for a woman was £3. The commission did not recommend any changes, suggesting that women did different jobs from men, so equal pay was not an issue. The male was still seen as the main breadwinner.

✘ The media continued to portray women in their traditional domestic role (see Source D).

Did you know?

By 1929, there were still 65,000 shell-shock victims from the First World War in psychiatric hospitals in Britain.

First World War and aftermath

During the war, the vast majority of casualties were those returning from the front and therefore medical facilities for civilians remained as they were and military hospitals were set up (see page 25). However, there were some triggers for change:

Triggers for change in health care

1 Poor health of lower classes

The war had highlighted poor health care and living conditions for the working classes – many people were shocked by the number of men who did not pass basic medical checks and were classed as 'unfit to fight' after they had volunteered.

2 Caring for the wounded

Most military hospitals had been set up as a temporary measure but many became permanent and continued to look after severely wounded and traumatised soldiers for many years after the war was over.

3 Global flu pandemic

1918 saw a global flu pandemic in which around a fifth of the world's population was infected. The virus swept through Britain with over 7,500 Britons dying from flu in the first week of November 1918 alone. This highlighted the lack of free hospital places. Most people were nursed in their homes, spreading the disease to family members.

4 Representation of the People Act, 1918

This increased the number of people who could vote. Many of the new voters did not have access to affordable health care. For example, this was the first time the government had to consider the health needs and wants of women.

Ministry of Health, 1919

In 1919 the government set up the Ministry of Health which gave the government an overview of health care provision across the UK. It also began to build some facilities such as TB hospitals.

The setting up of the Ministry of Health did lead to some improvement in the years between the wars. More hospitals were brought under the control of local authorities, secondary school pupils received free medical checks and health clinics were set up to give vaccinations cheaply. However, by 1939 health provision still largely depended on where you lived and how much money you had.

Second World War

The Second World War had a major impact on health provision both directly and indirectly:

- The medical requirements differed from the First World War because of the much greater numbers of civilians injured in bombing raids.

- The government set up a national Emergency Medical Service. All hospitals and medical staff were brought under control of the Ministry of Health, which provided free treatment (see page 31). This proved that government intervention could have a positive effect and people wanted a health service to continue after the war.

- For the first time, many people came into contact with poorer members of society (for example through evacuation) and were shocked at the poverty and lack of health care for these people.

Activity

10. Take each of the triggers for change in health care in the diagram and explain why they led to some change in the inter-war years.

The Beveridge Report of 1942 identified disease as one of the 'Five Giants' – the great social problems which needed to be addressed after the war (see page 42). Plans were made for a National Health Service (NHS), which was launched in 1948.

Taxes were used to pay for a wide range of free medical treatment including doctor's visits, hospital treatment, dentists and opticians and health care for pregnant women, children and the elderly.

At first, all treatment was free but because the NHS was so expensive, prescription charges were introduced in 1951. The NHS had a major impact on people's lives and particularly benefited poorer members of society who had previously been unable to afford medical care.

Activities

11. Create a priority ladder of factors which led to the creation of the NHS, with the most important reason at the top. Explain your decision.

12. Some people, especially doctors, were against the plans for a National Health Service. Why do you think this was the case?

A land fit for heroes? First World War reconstruction

A few days after the armistice, Prime Minister Lloyd George said: 'What is our task? To make Britain a fit country for heroes to live in.' He promised reform in many areas as part of his campaign for the 1918 election. When he was elected some limited reform took place but the Conservatives in the Coalition government would not allow anything more radical. Also, Britain was virtually bankrupt after the war and was soon in the depths of an **economic depression**. How much could be achieved?

Health

The government and wealthier classes had been shocked by the number of young men who were deemed unfit for war due to poor health. This was one of the reasons why the Ministry of Health was set up in 1919, which did make some attempts to improve health services.

Housing

At the end of the war there was an acute housing shortage. It was also acknowledged that poor-quality housing was partly responsible for the poor health of the working classes. In the inter-war years, 4 million new homes were built (1.5 million of them in the 1920s) by councils or with state subsidies. Many were built on the outskirts of towns – many suburbs developed. Many people were rehoused close to the city centres.

Education

The Education Act of 1918 raised the school leaving age to 14. It also introduced provision for children with special needs. Throughout the 1920s the interest in education was growing. Some of the Hadow Reports (1926, 1931 and 1933) led to changes in primary education and made important recommendations such as reducing class sizes.

What happened to the former soldiers?

Most soldiers wanted to return to their former lives as much as possible. Many did return to their original jobs although others were too young to have had jobs before they left for the front. For both, the economic depression and unemployment of the 1930s hit them hard. Former soldiers made up a large number of the unemployed and had to rely on soup kitchens and food distribution centres.

Wounded soldiers received disability payment from the army. However, this did not amount to a lot of money, especially if they were supporting a family and it was only for a limited time. Many found their disability allowance taken away from them before they were able to go out to work.

Activity

13. How true is it to say that Lloyd George's vision of 'a land fit for heroes' after the First World War was a total failure?

Economic depression: when trade drops, businesses fail and unemployment is increased.

Post-Second World War reconstruction, housing and welfare

The desire for change, for a better society, prompted the government to set up a Royal Commission in 1941 under Sir William Beveridge to consider how Britain could rebuild after the war. The Beveridge Report of 1942 recommended that the people of Britain should be protected from the 'Five Giant' evils: Squalor, Ignorance, Want, Idleness and Disease.

The Labour Party won the 1945 election with the promise that they would act on the Beveridge Report, which would help create a fairer, more equal society. However, by 1945 Britain was bankrupt after five years of total war – how much would the new government be able to achieve?

The setting up of the welfare state

The Labour Government of 1945–51 brought in reforms designed to remove the Five Giants identified by Beveridge. These reforms finally established a welfare state whereby the government took on the responsibility for helping those who could not help themselves.

The attack on want

The problem identified by Beveridge: a lack of basic needs such as food and clothing.

Actions: Family allowances began in 1945 with a payment for each child after the first. National Insurance against illness and unemployment was made compulsory and extended to the whole workforce.

The attack on disease

The problem identified by Beveridge: a lack of basic medical care for everyone.

Actions: In 1946 Aneurin Bevan, the Minister of Health, introduced the National Health Act. The National Health Service was launched in 1948 (see page 41).

The attack on ignorance

The problem identified by Beveridge: a lack of proper education for everyone.

Actions: The 1944 Education Act, brought in by Churchill's wartime government, introduced 'secondary education for all'. Children had to be taught in separate primary schools and secondary schools to replace the previous all age 'elementary' schools, and no one could leave school until the age of 15.

The attack on squalor

The problem identified by Beveridge: poor living conditions and lack of housing due to bombing and the lack of building during the Second World War.

Actions: The Labour Government built a series of estates of council houses. The New Towns Act of 1946 provided government money for a series of new towns close to London and other cities. These reduced overcrowding in older urban centres.

The attack on idleness

The problem identified by Beveridge: lack of employment opportunities.

Actions: Assistance from the USA (known as Marshall Aid) provided money and resources which the government used for new buildings and to restart industry. By 1950, the Labour Government had achieved almost full employment.

Activities

14. Design a poster to show how the introduction of the welfare state benefited men, women and children.
15. Which group of people benefited most from the welfare changes brought in after the Second World War. Explain your answer.

⚖ Your conclusion so far

In this topic you have examined the impact of the First and Second World wars on British society. You have:

- examined the changing social attitudes and the reasons for them
- evaluated the change in the role and status of women
- looked at the improvements in medical services brought about by the wars
- evaluated how far Britain was turned into a 'land fit for heroes' after the First World War
- examined post-war reconstruction in housing and welfare after 1945.

From what you have learned so far, how much change to society was brought about by war? To answer this question:

- describe the changes in society's attitudes to women, equality and the role of government
- assess how far the wars broke down barriers and undermined traditional views
- evaluate how much change actually remained after the wars.

Enquiry and writing skills support

Learning outcomes

By the end of this section, you should be able to:

- follow up an enquiry
- select and organise your material
- write up your enquiry.

In this section we will see how to complete the stages of following up an enquiry. The diagram on this page shows you the enquiry stages and what you need to do.

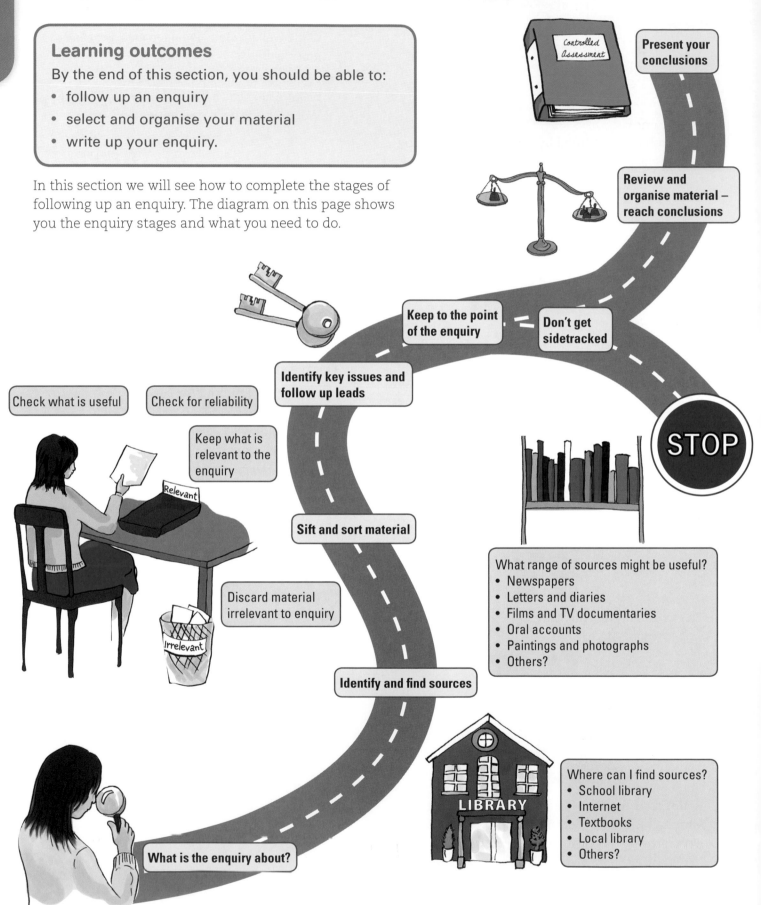

Present your conclusions

Review and organise material – reach conclusions

STOP

Keep to the point of the enquiry

Don't get sidetracked

Identify key issues and follow up leads

Check what is useful

Check for reliability

Keep what is relevant to the enquiry

Relevant

Sift and sort material

What range of sources might be useful?
- Newspapers
- Letters and diaries
- Films and TV documentaries
- Oral accounts
- Paintings and photographs
- Others?

Discard material irrelevant to enquiry

Irrelevant

Identify and find sources

LIBRARY

Where can I find sources?
- School library
- Internet
- Textbooks
- Local library
- Others?

What is the enquiry about?

Following up an enquiry 1: The impact of war on women's work c.1914–1919.

Your controlled assessment Part A task will be similar to this one:

> **Enquiry focus**
> Your enquiry task will focus on the change in women's working lives in the years 1914–1919.

In this practice example, we are going to follow up the enquiry focus. You will be able to use the skills you develop to follow up your own Part A enquiry.

What is this enquiry about?

Your first step is to identify the precise enquiry. In this instance it is asking you to compare working lives before, during and immediately after the First World War.

This enquiry is trying to find out:

- what jobs women had during the war and whether this was different from before
- what pay and conditions were like for women workers during this period and whether this was different from before
- how permanent these changes were (whether they continued after the war was over).

Identify and find sources

The next stage is to gather your information. Start with an easy outline book and read through the relevant material. Write some summary notes, making sure you include the book title, author and the pages where you have found the information. You should only start to look for more in-depth information when you have used two or three textbooks which give you the basic information.

Begin by rereading pages 7, 10 and 26 of this book and completing the activities on this page.

Activities

Making notes

1. Make a bullet point list of useful information from your first source of information. For example:
   - Before the First World War, women who did work were confined to certain jobs such as domestic service (mostly as lady's maids or kitchen hands), the textile industry, nursing or teaching girls.
   - The war saw women enter new industries such as engineering and manufacturing for the first time.

2. Now repeat this process for two other textbooks or simple overviews.

3. Begin to organise your notes. You could sort them into a table like the one below.

	Work done by women
Pre-war	
During war	
Post war	

Add to your sources

You might start by doing a quick search on the internet but remember that many internet sites are just opinions without any factual support. You should also look at books by historians. When you find a book check the contents page and the index to make sure it covers the topic you want to research. For this enquiry you could look up 'women's war work', 'employment', 'munitions workers' and so on.

You could also use television documentaries as a source of information but be careful to check them against other sources to be sure they have not been too dramatised or exaggerated.

Sift and sort material

Go through your new sources and make additional notes. It will help if you use a fresh page for each book or other source of information. Remember that the book or the webpage you've found was not written to answer your specific question. For example, this enquiry is about: the changes in women's work during and immediately after the First World War. You have to choose what to take from your source to answer that – see activities 1 and 4.

Look for new leads to follow up. For example, Source A tells you that women replaced men in office work with few troubles but there were difficulties in getting employers in manufacturing industries to accept women.

As you identify new leads, you can follow them up, going through the same process of finding, sifting and sorting, and noting information.

ResultsPlus
Top Tip

Looking for information can be a slow process. You might read through a lot to get a small piece of new information. But your work is better if you concentrate on what's new and relevant, rather than adding something that repeats information you already have or is not relevant.

Stick to the enquiry path

Don't go off track! On a journey, detours and side roads can be great fun and you can follow them up just because they are interesting. Remember, though, to return to your enquiry path – and not to add in material which isn't relevant. For example, information on the campaign for the vote for women does not provide relevant details for an enquiry into women's working lives.

Activities

Selecting information

4. Read Source A and decide with a partner how much of it would be useful for this enquiry. Remember:

   - you want to find out what changed in work done by women during the war and what stayed the same

   - usually you want only new points

   - sometimes you may want to make a note that two sources agree about an important point.

5. Copy the whole source. Colour-code it: green for new information and blue for repeated information. Some parts have been done for you.

Source A: An extract from *GCSE Modern World History* by Ben Walsh and Christopher Culpin.

By early 1916, Britain had up to 2 million workers fewer than were necessary to keep the country going.

In offices the absence of men did not pose a particular problem. Women were soon employed in place of the male clerks who joined up, and by the end of the war half a million women had replaced men in office jobs. Government departments employed a further 200,000 female clerks.

In manufacturing, however, it was a different story, at least to start with. Employers were very reluctant to take on women to fill men's jobs. They thought that women would not learn the necessary skills, and also feared trouble from the unions. In fact, the unions did resist the employment of women workers, fearing that women would be paid less and that this would be a threat to men's wages. Most unions did not even accept female members.

By 1916, the shortage of engineering workers was desperate, especially as more and more munitions and supplies, and increasing numbers of men were needed at the front. For practical reasons, employers were persuaded to take on women workers. The government set an example to private industry by employing women almost exclusively in its own munitions factories. By the end of the war, almost 800,000 women had taken up work in engineering industries. The evidence soon showed that even with very little training they were as skilled as men.

Using sources carefully

So far we have applied two tests when using sources – relevance and duplication. Sometimes you will also need to think about reliability. You need to be particularly careful about internet sources because they are sometimes anonymous and it is difficult to check the information they contain. Remember that many internet sites are just opinions without any factual support.

With any source, think about purpose and possible bias. As you use your sources, apply the RDR tests: **R**elevance, **D**uplication and **R**eliability.

Activities

Relevance and reliability

6. Study Source B. It was written by the daughter of a very famous American campaigner for women's rights.

7. Decide with a partner which of these statements you agree with. Choose as many as you like:
   - It is not biased.
   - It is biased but still has some useful information.
   - It is mainly relevant to this enquiry.
   - It does not add much to this enquiry.

8. Add any useful information to your notes.

Source B: An extract from *Mobilizing Woman-Power* by Harriot Stanton Blatch, 1918.

> When Great Britain recognized that the war could not be won [only by soldiers at] the front…she began to build an efficient organization of industry at home.
>
> British women gave instant response to the call for labor-power. In munitions a million are mobilized, in the Land Army over 300,000 have been drafted [conscripted] and actually placed on the farms, and in the Women's Army Auxiliary Corps 14,000 women are working in direct connection with the fighting force, and an additional 10,000 are being called out for service each month. In the clerical force of the government departments, some of which had never seen women before in their sacred precincts, over 180,000 are now working. And the women civil servants are not only engaged in indoor service, but outside too, most of the carrying of mail being in their hands.
>
> Women are dock-laborers, some 7,000 strong. 4,000 act as patrols and police, 40,000 are in banks and various financial houses…

ResultsPlus

Top Tip

Remember when you think about the impact of the war on women's work in 1914–19, the impact changes as the war goes on and changes again when the conflict stops.

Identify key issues and follow up leads

Activities

9. Study Source C in the source file on the next page. It gives two new leads: the drop in the number of employed women at the start of the war and the movement of women from some industries to others.

10. Add information from Source C to your notes. In your real enquiry, it will help if you add page numbers as you build up your notes, in case you want to find the passage again.

11. Begin to organise your information under key headings whenever you use a new source.

    So far this enquiry has provided the following leads. The words in bold could be used as headings.
    - **New types of work** were opened up to women.
    - **Office and clerical work** quickly became 'acceptable' employment for women.
    - **Engineering and manufacturing** took longer to become accepted and then only temporarily.

ResultsPlus

Top Tip

When you make statements about change, always back them up precisely and make comparisons using words such as 'before…, but in…, however after…'.

Source file

Source C: From *All Quiet on the Home Front,* Richard Van Emden and Steve Humphries, 2003.

[In the early months of the war] in the world of paid work, many jobs that traditionally employed women were axed, such as in the garment industry, the fishing industry (where women were employed as fish gutters), and among confectionery makers. In all, some one in seven women lost their jobs and charities were set up to find them employment. Those industries that had shaken out almost half a million male workers during the first days of the war were traditionally male-dominated; when they later looked to refill the vacancies they would consider only other men, not women. As the unions had yet to agree to giving jobs to women, they gravitated towards the secretarial and clerical posts vacated by men enlisting; indeed, 50 per cent more women were to work in white-collar jobs during the war than in industry and agriculture.

Source D: The views of a historian writing in 1996, quoted in *War and the transformation of British Society,* Nigel Kelly.

In 1914 a woman's place was in the home. Should she need to work, then suitable occupations were decided by men. The First World War was nothing more than a temporary victory. Women had never been welcome in 'men's jobs' and the belief that their presence devalued skills was never overcome. A mixture of threat and incentive ensured that women returned to their 'proper place' and stayed there – until another war demanded their services.

Source E: From *Women and Work in Wartime Britain,* Deborah Thom.

As early as November 1914, there was some expansion in employment opportunities, the greatest in clerical and shop assistant work. [This] had been under way before the war, but the numbers of clerical staff were to increase further due to increased volume of paper work. Most women taken on were not replacements but extra workers. Finally, and most importantly, this 'feminisation' [increase of women workers] aroused no social concerns. Office and shop work was clean, respectable and presented no obvious threat to [women's] health…Very few women did in fact do very much new 'unsuitable work. Most were to work throughout the war on work defined as 'women's work'. Those who did undertake heavy, outdoor work were explicitly there for the duration only.

Source F: From *War and the transformation of British society,* 2009 by Nigel Kelly.

…during the war, five million men joined the army and women had to step into their places to keep the country going. Women took on jobs such as bus conductors, drivers or workers on the railways. But attitudes take time to change. Even the government seemed slow to realise how important women were in helping the country fight the war. It took until March 1915 for it to draw up a register of women willing to undertake work. Even then, not all those women were given work. In frustration, the suffragettes organised a demonstration in London in July 1915 demanding the 'Right to Serve'.

For many middle-class women, the employment opportunities provided by the war brought them a new independence. For the first time they were financially independent from their husbands. Many working-class women were already used to working, but the wages in the new jobs were often considerably higher than those they had earned before the war. Although women remained very much in the minority in the work force, and were usually paid less than men, the war did bring a significant change in attitudes. Women began to wear more make-up, visit pubs, buy their own drinks and even wear trousers! Although after the war many women lost their jobs when the men returned, a significant step on the road to equality had been taken.

Source G: Percentage of jobs held by women in various areas of employment in Britain 1914–18.

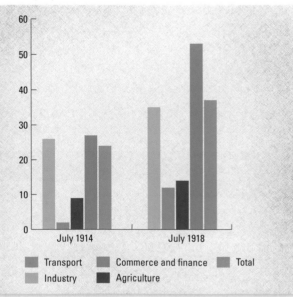

Source H: From *Women on the Home Front in World War One,* Professor Joanna Bourke.

The war…opened up a wider range of occupations to female workers and hastened the collapse of traditional women's employment, particularly domestic service. From the 19th century to 1911, between 11 and 13 per cent of the female population in England and Wales were domestic servants. By 1931, the percentage had dropped to under eight per cent…working women who might previously have been enticed into service were being drawn away by alternative employment opening up to satisfy the demands of war. Thus, nearly half of the first recruits to the London General Omnibus Company in 1916 were former domestic servants. Clerical work was another draw card. The number of women in the Civil Service increased from 33,000 in 1911 to 102,000 by 1921. The advantages of these alternative employments over domestic service were obvious: wages were higher, conditions better, and independence enhanced.

However, the war did not inflate women's wages. Employers [got around] wartime equal pay regulations by employing several women to replace one man, or by dividing skilled tasks into several less skilled stages. In these ways, women could be employed at a lower wage and not said to be 'replacing' a man directly. By 1931, a working woman's weekly wage had returned to the pre-war situation of being half the male rate in more industries.

Source I: From an article in *The Times*, 1 March 1919.

Women in dockyards: more dismissals

Numbers of women who were engaged for work of various kinds in the Royal dockyards during the war are being discharged now that the men whose places they filled are returning from active service.

Some protests have been made against the…notices of dismissal, but generally it is recognised that the employment of the women was temporary…It is pointed out, however, that the discharge of widows of dockyard and naval men will involve hardship in some instances, because many of these women have children dependent upon them; and recently, at a meeting of the Portsmouth branch of an ex-Service men's organization, a resolution was passed condemning the discharge of 'war widows' from Government establishments.

Follow up more leads

At this stage in your enquiry, you will have a number of leads. You now need to follow them up, using the source file and any other sources you have found. Look back at page 44 to keep yourself on track. Review your material – can you identify any gaps which you need to research? What are the key areas that you should go into in more depth?

Review and organise material – reach conclusions

Finally you will need to reach a conclusion. In this example you should decide on the amount of change in working lives of women between 1914 and 1919. You could summarise your key points in an ideas map or in timelines. For example, some types of work, such as engineering, were opened up to women for the war years only, whereas other types of work, such as office work, remained open to women once the war was over.

You have discovered that the First World War opened up new opportunities for women in work. Some of these became permanent while others were only temporary. Similarly, while pay and conditions did improve for some women, for many they did not change.

Present your conclusions

This activity is practice writing for your controlled assessment task. After you have completed the activity you could turn to Maximise your marks on page 72 to see if your answer could be improved.

Activities

12. Make a set of notes to go with your ideas map. Use the same headings. Do not use more than two sides of paper. You can include quotations from your sources in your notes but make sure you explain why they are important.

13. Write up your enquiry: how much change was there in the working lives of women 1914–19?

Following up an enquiry 2:
Reasons for improvements in health and welfare provision after the Second World War

This practice enquiry is different from enquiry 1. Enquiry 1 asked you how working lives changed during the war. This enquiry is asking 'why' something happened.

For this you need to find reasons why health and welfare services improved after the Second World War. Follow the enquiry stages outlined on page 44. Identify, sift and sort your information.

Begin by using page 34 and pages 42–43 of this book. Then go on to the information given in the source file opposite. You can then follow up more leads if you like.

Don't forget to stick to the enquiry path when you follow up your leads, and remember the RDR tests (page 46).

In enquiries such as this one, which asks for reasons, students often make the mistake of simply describing reasons. You must link the information you find out to reasons why this led to improvements. For example, don't just say that 'rationing treated everyone equally' but explain that 'rationing treated everyone equally and so people wanted this idea of equality to continue after the war'.

Activities

Making and sorting notes

14. Make a bullet point list of useful information, for example:
    - Evacuation highlighted poverty and inequality as country people came into contact with children from inner cities.
    - The Emergency Medical Service showed the benefits of a nationally organised system of health care.

15. Begin to organise your notes. You could arrange them into a chart like the one shown here. Notes have been started for you but add new bullet points for each heading. You can add more headings if you need to.

Evacuation
• People were shocked by the ill health of some evacuees, usually caused by lack of food and poor living conditions.
• Poverty was also highlighted as some evacuees had only one set of clothes and no shoes.
• Evacuees came into contact with better living conditions and sanitation.
German bombing
• Increased medical needs
•
Rationing
•
Role of government
•
Beveridge Report
•

16. Now colour code your chart. Use green to highlight points which show attitudes were changing and red for policies during the war which set an example for the welfare state.

Source file

Source A: An extract from *GCSE Modern World History* by Ben Walsh and Christopher Culpin.

The Second World War had a major effect on attitudes. To begin with, there was the need to treat large numbers of civilian casualties from German bombing raids. This gave many people access to health care which they had never had before. There was a general feeling of unity within the nation, and also a sense that when war ended a new era would begin. Also, during the war, the state controlled almost every aspect of people's lives, and so the idea of the government looking after citizens' health did not seem strange.

Source B: An extract from *War and the transformation of British society* by Jane Shuter.

On 1 December 1942, the Beveridge report, over 300 pages long, was published. Many MPs (most of them Conservative) disagreed strongly with its recommendations, but realised it had a huge amount of public support. It sold over 70,000 copies in the first few days.

The report said that the state should support its citizens 'from the cradle to the grave' – from birth until death…

As the government took control of more and more aspects of life during the war, it changed people's views on how government worked and what parts of life it was responsible for. Even Conservative MPs saw it would be harder to avoid welfare responsibilities once the war was over…There was overwhelming agreement that the Beveridge plan should be put into effect…

Source C: Part of a speech by Winston Churchill in London on 9 November 1943.

I regard it as a definite part of the responsibility of this National Government to have policies perfected to make sure that in the years immediately after the war, food, work and homes are found for all. The war would not be won unless there was a policy of food, work and homes after victory for the men and women who fought and won.

Source D: An extract from the National Health Service History website.

The Beveridge Report…aimed for universal coverage, and named 'five giants' on the road to reconstruction: want, disease, ignorance, squalor and idleness. The depression in the 1920s and 1930s, the lack of systematic provision for health care at that time, the experience of communal action in war and the efficiency of the EMS all pointed to the need for a health service…

The war had increased the sense of social solidarity, and many saw the advantages of a command structure. Most doctors had military experience and knew that [soldiers] had, from a health point of view, been looked after better than in peacetime…As early as 1943 the Ministry of Health was considering the transition of the wartime EMS into a comprehensive health service, free and available to all.

Source E: An extract from 'What Britain thinks of The Beveridge Report' as shown by a Gallup Poll by the British Institute of Public Opinion in 1942–3.

Great interest in the Report was discovered and, strikingly enough, this interest was most marked amongst the poorer people.

General approval was found for the main features of the schemes as set out in the Report. The extent of the approval varied from a bare majority saying that weekly benefits of 40s. per week for a married couple was about the right amount, to an overwhelming endorsement of [agreement with] the proposal to include everyone in a comprehensive scheme of medical services.

Source F: From *Britain in the Second World War* by Mark Donnelly, 1999.

[Some historians think that] evacuation played a major role in the promotion of [equality] as town met country and working class met middle class. [This] increased national awareness of the problem of urban poverty, as reception halls across the country filled up with apparently malnourished [under fed] and lice-ridden children, lacking clothing and displaying little if any evidence of schooling. Stories about poverty-stricken evacuees filled the local and national press, speeches were made in parliament about the need to tackle the serious social problems highlighted by evacuation and the Prime Minister, Chamberlain promised that… action would be taken. According to [the historian] Titmuss, evacuation stirred the national conscience and produced important changes in social policy…

Source G: From an article, 'The Hardship of Rationing', from a web source about the home front in the Second World War.

The Minister of Food, Lord Woolton, offered novelty food suggestions such as…recipes like Woolton Pie, carrot fudge, poor man's goose and sultana casserole. He also ensured every child under the age of three received daily milk, cod liver oil and orange juice to boost their vitamin intake and those under five, cod liver oil. Free school meals were also allocated to those children of poorer families.

Despite the British people having to go without, on the whole rationing did mean that the nation was much better fed than it had been in the 1930s. People preferred equality to a free for all in which the 'well-off' would stockpile food and the poor go hungry.

Undoubtedly while everyone was hungry in wartime Britain, no one starved.

Writing up your answer

The moderator will be looking for four main things – that you have:

- kept your answer focused on the enquiry
- found information from different sources
- backed up your statements with information
- communicated your answer by organising it well and using good spelling, punctuation and grammar.

The activities which follow will help you to improve your writing. Remember to use the skills you have learned when you write up your controlled assessment answer.

Activities

Improving writing

17. Study examples 1 and 2 on page 53, imagining you are the moderator. Discuss with a partner the good and bad points of each example. You will find the answers at the bottom of the page.

18. Suggest ways you could improve examples 1 and 2. You can do this in bullet point notes.

19. Study example 3. It is part of a high-level response. It gives several reasons and supports them with precise information from sources. Now try adding to the answer by giving examples to support the last statement. You can also add more paragraphs giving other reasons.

ResultsPlus
Top Tip

Students who can show how factors link will do well in Part A of their Controlled Assessment. Think about the links between changing attitudes in wartime, government actions in wartime and the improvement after the war.

The reasons for improvements in health and welfare provision after the Second World War

Example extract 1

In the Second World War, the government took control of people's lives more and when the war ended people wanted this to continue as they realised it could make their lives better. Evacuation showed rich people how poor some people were so they wanted the government to do something about it.

Example extract 2

The Second World War changed people's attitudes towards poverty and healthcare. Lots of people were injured in the Blitz and the government took over all hospitals and gave people free health care which they liked. The Beveridge Report was published in 1942 and this recommended that a National Health Service was set up which gave everyone free healthcare all the time. The general public really liked this idea. The NHS was set up in 1948 and meant that everyone could see doctors, opticians and dentists free of charge. This had a major impact on people's health and was very popular. It particularly helped the poorest people as many of them had been unable to afford professional healthcare in the past.

Example extract 3

The Second World War helped to raise awareness of the inequalities and poverty in Britain. The government introduced rationing of food, clothes and other goods such as petrol. This meant that rich and poor had the same rations, which people approved of because it was seen as fair. While some had less than they were used to, other people's health improved and, as the Home Sweet Home Front website notes, 'on the whole rationing did mean that the nation was much better fed than it had been in the 1930s'.

The policy of evacuation meant that many inner-city children were sent to live in the countryside in wealthier homes. For the first time, many middle-class and wealthy people became aware of the poverty in the cities and were shocked by underfed children with illnesses caused by poor housing and healthcare. Mark Donelly in *Britain in the Second World War* points out that stories of 'poverty-stricken' evacuees were widely reported in the press and led to speeches being made in parliament promising improvement once the war was over. Evacuation also meant that many children from poor families found out about things like proper toilets which highlighted how bad their lives had been. This meant that more people wanted things to change.

The role of government was greatly expanded in the wars. This had two major effects which led to improvements in health and welfare after the war. Firstly, there were several government actions during the war which continued and were expanded after the war. For example, the government took control of all hospitals to deal with the casualties from enemy bombs and gave all young children free milk and orange juice to make sure they were healthy. Secondly, and perhaps more importantly, it became acceptable for the government to have a greater role in people's lives
[answer gives examples, quoting sources].

Summary

Success in your enquiry comes from:

- sticking to the focus of the enquiry

- using a range of sources, keeping their relevance and reliability in mind

- organising your answer to show good quality of written communication.

Part B Representations of history

How did civilians respond to the Blitz?

> ### Learning outcomes
>
> By the end of this chapter, you should be able to:
>
> • know about some of the different reactions to the Blitz
> • understand that people have different views about how civilians responded to bombing attacks
> • understand why there are different views about how well civilians coped.

In Part B of your controlled assessment you are exploring different ideas about the Blitz. At the time there were different views on how well people were coping, just as there are today. The aim of this chapter is to explore this issue and understand why historians' views about the Blitz also differ.

Reactions to the Blitz

Advances in technology meant that bombing raids on British cities were very destructive. The raids that began on 7 September 1940 went on to affect cities across all parts of the United Kingdom. The main target was, of course, the capital, London. For example 12,500 people were killed there in December 1940 alone. The attacks spread from Plymouth in the south west, to Southampton as well as Coventry, Liverpool, Glasgow and Belfast, among others.

At the time, certain beliefs about the character and qualities of British people during the Blitz became popular.

British people were seen as:

• angry but not broken
• not bothered about a person's class or background as long as the war was won

• willing to make sacrifices
• brave in the face of suffering
• keen to pull together and remain united
• cheerful and willing to take it 'on the chin'
• deserving of victory
• uniquely resilient – able to cope with all the hardship.

Activities

1. Are any of the qualities listed above still seen as uniquely British today?

Source A shows bomb damage to Buckingham Palace with the royal family in the foreground. Photographs like this were released to encourage support for the war. The government wanted to ensure that the message got through that everyone was suffering and should therefore remain strong and determined to win the war.

Source A: King George VI and Queen Elizabeth outside bomb-damaged Buckingham Palace in 1940.

There are many reasons why historians find it challenging to reach an objective view about how British civilians coped during the Blitz.

The sources historians have to use to carry out this enquiry are questionable. Potential evidence about the Blitz is influenced by:

- patriotism
- romanticising the past
- censorship and propaganda.

Patriotism

This means that some people are keen to represent the efforts of civilians as brave and heroic. Making negative comments about people during wartime could be seen as an unnecessary criticism of your country.

Romanticising the past

This means that some people are keen to remember the war years in a positive way. Perhaps this is because focusing on the suffering is too painful, or they might want to believe that the suffering was worth it.

Censorship and propaganda

This means that the Ministry of Information had control over what people knew about the attacks and presented the events in certain ways. For example, many pictures of damaged housing and dead bodies were not approved for publication.

Activities

2. Study Source B. What might it suggest about how people coped in the Blitz?
3. Would the British government be keen to release images like this?
4. Which of the popular ideas about the British people listed on page 54 does it convey? Explain your choice.

Source B: A milkman delivering milk in a London street devastated during a German bombing raid. Firemen are dampening down the ruins behind him.

ResultsPlus
Top Tip

Sometimes sources point the reader in a particular direction but students who do well look at other related sources to understand them more fully. Look for example, at sources B and C together.

Source C: An extract from *The Times* newspaper on 3 July, 2007.

On the morning of October 10, 1940, a photograph taken by Fred Morley…was published in a London newspaper…This was the morning after a German air raid. Walking gamely over the rubble that filled the frame, the milkman was a symbol of British pluck and determination… What readers did not know was that the milkman was actually Fred Morley's assistant, persuaded to dress up as a milkman…Censors at the Ministry of Information would have suppressed images of large-scale destruction for fear of eroding morale, but Morley got round this with a little subterfuge.

We can see from Sources B and C that some evidence is questionable. Only by looking at these two sources together can you reach a fuller understanding of how people reacted to the bombing raids and how the government controlled access to information and therefore shaped public opinion.

In the next section you will explore how evidence can point in different directions and consider how this affects historians' judgements. We will focus on the following questions about the impact of the Blitz.

- How far did people try to carry on with life as normal?
- To what degree did people manage to unite in the face of these difficulties?

- Was morale kept high or were the British people near despair?
- How effectively did the government provide protection for civilians?

These are all contested issues and therefore lead to differences between historians. This will help us understand how judgements can sometimes be difficult for the range of reasons explained on the previous page.

By examining these questions we will be able to see that the evidence points in different directions when we ask: *Is 'Blitz spirit' myth or reality?*

Also, because people's attitudes and values differ, historians, as people themselves, sometimes reach different conclusions from the sources they use. This can happen even when the sources they use are the same.

Activities

5. What do Sources B and C suggest about the effectiveness of government censorship?

6. On the next two pages there are four pairs of sources, grouped under the headings: How normal? How united? High morale? Effective government protection? Analyse each pair of sources and spot similarities and differences in how different people reacted to the Blitz. You could use a table like this to help organise your ideas.

	Sources D and E How normal?	Sources F and G How united?	Sources H and I High morale?	Sources J and K Effective government protection?
Similarities between the sources				
Differences between the sources				
Your judgement	Both D and E show people attempting to carry on life as usual although in very difficult circumstances. The war meant that relationships developed more quickly and practical problems like shortages and separation led to couples getting married. Source D suggests that society was more accepting of people marrying quickly in the war years.			

How normal?

Source D: Irene Harris was living in Plymouth. She was interviewed about her experiences for the book, *Voices from the Past: The Blitz* (1987).

Matt, my boyfriend… had nowhere to live and everybody's nerves were stretched so we decided to get married…You could get married quickly in those days. The registry office had been bombed. All the windows were gone as well as half the house. The room we got married in had a rough wooden table and a few odd chairs. Most of the guests had to stand. It wasn't a bit like a wedding…We were married on 21st May, 1941, and the following September 10th, Matt got called up. I only saw him a few times after that until the war ended.

Source E: A photograph of a wedding ceremony taking place among the ruins of a bombed church in London, October 1940.

How united?

Source F: An extract from *Very Little Luggage* (2009) by Kenneth Sinclair-Loutit.

…together we developed a number of very effective techniques for extracting casualties and helping to save lives… They were wonderful people in the East End of London, they were consistently admirable. Someone in 1991 has written a book to say that…the Blitz was exaggerated so that we could all give ourselves a self-satisfying ego-trip. I am sorry that this author did not share our lives during that period.

Source G: An extract from 'Germany Calling' (29 August, 1940). William Joyce broadcast anti-British propaganda from Germany. The announcements began with the phase, 'Germany calling'. They urged the British people to surrender and aimed to lower British morale. It became popular listening in Britain as many people were keen to find out information about the enemy and what they were saying about Britain.

There were two Londons that night. Down by the docks and in the poor districts and the suburbs, people lay dead, or dying in agony from their wounds; but, while their counterparts were suffering only a little distance away…the [privileged rich] were making the raid an excuse for their drunken orgies…in the saloons of Piccadilly and in the Cafe de Paris. Spending on champagne in one night what they would consider enough for a soldier's wife for a month these monied fools shouted and sang in the streets, crying…'They won't bomb this part of the town! They want the docks! Fill up boys!'

High morale?

Source H: Harry Meacham worked as an air-raid warden. He was interviewed for the television documentary 'The People's War' (1987).

> ...people were walking over heads that had been blown off bodies. We brought out forty people on pieces of corrugated sheets. We used anything we could find. I remember bringing out one fellow who had lost his face down one side. His arm was gone. His leg was gone. He looked up at me and said: 'Have you got a cigarette, mate?' I lit it up for him and put it in his lips. He took a couple of puffs and said: 'Will you tell me landlady I shall not be home to tea.' And with that he closed his eyes and was gone.

Source I: Anthony Cruikshank remembers life in Liverpool during the Blitz – from the BBC website 'Local history Liverpool'.

> I suppose the **communiqués** had to be misleading so as not to give the enemy too much to gloat about. But the fact remains that the **traumatised** people of Liverpool were dangerously close to **capitulation**.

Effective government protection?

Source J: Muriel Simkin worked in a munitions factory in Dagenham during the Second World War. She was interviewed about her experiences for the book, *Voices from the Past: The Blitz* (1987).

> Sometimes the Germans would drop their bombs before the second bell went. On one occasion a bomb hit the factory before we were given permission to go to the shelter. The paint department went up. I saw several people flying through the air and I just ran home. I was suffering from shock. I was suspended for six weeks without pay. They would have been saved if they had been allowed to go after the first alarm. It was a terrible job but we had no option. We all had to do war work. We were risking our lives in the same way as the soldiers were.

Communiqués: official reports often sent in a hurry.

Traumatised: psychologically deeply upset as a result of a bad experience – in this case the bombing raids.

Capitulation: the act of surrendering or giving up.

Source K: Winston Churchill, the prime minister, walking through the remains of Coventry Cathedral, which had been bombed, in 1942.

58

Activities

Is the Blitz spirit myth or reality?

Blitz spirit   Blitz despair

7. A tug of war team needs to be strong and well linked, so that it pulls well. Create your 'teams' by adding points which give strength to each 'side'. Complete each of the following sentences using the 'strengthening points' below. Link the argument more tightly choosing from the 'linking words' or by using words of your own.

Remember to refer back to the table you completed and use examples from the sources to extend the strengthening points with your own ideas.

- The evidence suggests…
- British civilians showed Blitz spirit because…
- British civilians showed Blitz despair because…

Strengthening points

War work was accepted by people in cities as making their contribution to win the war.

Getting married during the war was an act of faith that you had a future.

The prime minister made great efforts to keep people feeling positive.

The Ministry of Information was selective about releasing very bad news.

Some districts were on the edge of collapse and civil unrest.

People got used to suffering and accepted it as necessary.

Rich and poor suffered in unequal measures.

Many people were willing to risk their lives to help others in dangerous situations.

Some people were desperate for the authorities to end the war at any cost.

Linking words

- Also
- Additionally
- Furthermore
- Similarly
- Therefore
- As a result

8. Decide which argument is stronger overall and give your reasons.

9. Take a vote with other class members. You could develop this further into a class debate.

10. Write up your discussions to explore why views of the reaction to the Blitz differ. You can use the fact file to extend your answer.

Fact file

- The king and queen were photographed outside Buckingham Palace after it had been damaged in a raid on 10 September 1940.
- 2 million Anderson shelters were provided by the government in the early months of the war.
- In September 1940 the government opened up 80 stations across the London Underground after public pressure to do so.
- By June 1941, 43,000 civilians had been killed and 1.5 million homes lost due to bombing raids.
- During 1944–45 guided missiles were used in raids. About 500 V2s hit London. They could not be shot down or seen because they flew at supersonic speed.

Summary

- Historians have different views about how civilians reacted to the Blitz on British towns and cities.
- This is because the evidence is problematic and points in different directions.
- Judgements can be difficult to reach because people, including historians, often have different attitudes and values and therefore hold different opinions or view things in different ways.

Understanding and analysing representations of history

Learning outcomes

By the end of this topic, you should be able to:

- understand what is meant by representations of history
- understand how historical representations are created
- analyse representations and judge how far they differ from one another.

What are representations of history?

A representation of history is a depiction of the past created visually or in words. It is designed to create an image of things in the past – an event, a movement, the role of an individual, and so on. Historians create representations when they write about the past. They create a picture of what life was like, why people acted as they did and what the consequences of events and developments were. Novelists, filmmakers and cartoonists also give us an image of past societies and events. In each case, the way they show their subject creates a representation of it.

Analysing representations

Someone who creates a representation takes some of the same steps you might take when creating a Facebook entry or taking a photograph. You choose what you are taking a photograph of or how to show yourself. Do you want to record an important event? Will you show it as happy or solemn? Do you want to show the beauty of a particular place? To get the effect you want, you choose which things to focus on. Sometimes you decide to leave things out. You make decisions about how to show the scene or the event.

When you analyse a representation you should look at each part separately and think about how it affects the overall image. From the details you can infer (work out) what impression the artist or author is trying to give.

A modern example of a representation

Let's first take a modern image and use the same skills needed to analyse a historical representation. Study Source A below.

Source A: An illustration from the website of the British Tourist Board, 2009. It shows a scene on the east coast of England.

| Inclusion of the boat and the windmill. | Blue sky: would the photograph have been taken on a rainy day? | Uncrowded scene: no objects in the centre of the picture. | Happy-looking young couple: do people look happy all the time? Why has the photographer not shown just one person alone? |

Note the details the photographer has chosen to include. Why have these details been included? What messages are they designed to give? Can you suggest anything which may have been deliberately left out? What do you think is the purpose of the representation in Source A?

Now study Source B. It is a photograph taken in the middle of an August morning. It shows a part of the coast near to the place shown in Source A. The building in the background is a nuclear power station.

Source B: A holiday photograph taken at Sizewell on the Suffolk coast, August 2009.

Which parts of Source A are supported by details in Source B? Would you use Source B to advertise holidays on the Suffolk coast? If not, why not? If yes, which parts of the photograph would you select?

Source A is not *inaccurate*, but Source B helps to show us that Source A is not a *complete* representation. Source A is one view and, when we analyse it, we can infer the message and purpose of this representation from the choices the photographer has made. Source A is designed to portray the coast as attractive and uncrowded, a place to enjoy walks and be happy. Its purpose is to encourage people to take holidays in the area.

Activity

1. Describe the representation of the east coast of England given in Source A. Use details from Source A. You could begin: 'Source A is a representation of the east coast. It is designed to portray it as…We can tell this because…'

Try to use most of the following words and phrases in your description (you can use them in any order):

- selected
- chosen to
- omitted
- deliberately
- highlighted
- included
- incomplete.

You can also use details from Source B if you wish.

A case study in historical representations: the Bethnal Green underground station disaster

Source C: At the southeast entrance to Bethnal Green tube station you can find this small commemorative plaque.

> SITE OF THE WORST CIVILIAN DISASTER
> OF THE SECOND WORLD WAR
>
> IN MEMORY OF
> 173 MEN, WOMEN AND CHILDREN
> WHO LOST THEIR LIVES ON THE
> EVENING OF WEDNESDAY 3RD MARCH 1943
> DESCENDING THESE STEPS TO BETHNAL GREEN
> UNDERGROUND AIR RAID SHELTER
>
> NOT FORGOTTEN

Countdown to disaster at Bethnal Green

Heavy British bombing of Berlin on 1 March meant people in the East End of London were expecting a retaliatory strike on 3 March. Those people whose local shelter was Bethnal Green were getting prepared.

↓

By early evening, 500 people were getting settled in for the night in the shelter at Bethnal Green.

↓

At 8.17pm the warning sirens began and up to 1,500 further people descended into the shelter down a dimly lit staircase.

↓

At 8.27pm a terrifying and unfamiliar roar was heard as people tried desperately to get into the safety of the shelter from street level.

↓

A crowd pushed forward and a woman holding a child fell at the bottom of the stairway. This led to horrifying consequences in the crush that followed.

↓

The authorities tried to keep the disaster secret, which made rescue attempts even more difficult.

↓

In this disaster, 173 people died: 62 children, 84 women and 27 men.

ResultsPlus
Top Tip

Always remember that artists or authors make choices about what to put in their representations. That will help you to analyse the representation they have created.

Activities

2. How would you design a memorial to remember those who suffered in this tragedy?
3. Which of the following themes would you emphasise?

- Sacrifice
- Innocence
- Gratefulness to rescuers.

Analysing memorials as representations

Plans for a new memorial have been proposed by survivors and their families. The computer visualisation in Source D shows what it will look like. It will include the names and ages of the victims and additional plaques telling the stories of those connected to the disaster.

When we construct a memorial we are deciding how an event should be represented. We make judgements about why that event is significant in order to decide what to include and how we want that event to be remembered.

Source D: The proposed memorial at Bethnal Green tube station. This memorial encourages people to remember events in a particular way.

The upside-down stairway represents the space where the people died

The name 'stairway to heaven' suggests that good people died.

The extra plaques tell the stories of the people who died and those who tried to help them.

Copyright of visualisation by Arboreal Architecture (local Bethnal Green architect who designed the memorial).

The memorial plaques encourage the living to think about the lives lost.

The suspended stairs cannot be walked on as they are beyond the reach of the living.

To understand more completely what happened at Bethnal Green we can also look at personal accounts about events that night (see sources E and F).

Source E: A survivor, 'Mrs B', quoted as part of the official enquiry held into the disaster.

There were torches flashing, they were not police officers because someone called out over our heads and the baby was free...I had my hand on the baby and said, 'Will you please take the baby?' and he said, 'Every man for himself at a time like this'.

Source F: A quotation from Doris Russell, who was a student nurse at Bethnal Green Hospital.

We were waiting in the Outpatients' Department for the ambulances and casualties to arrive. The few beds were soon taken up and stretchers had to be left on the floor. The ambulance personnel were shocked, as also were the hospital staff, doctors and nurses, as there were no visible signs of injuries. No wounds, no broken bones, nor crying or exclamations of pain. All were pronounced DOA (dead on arrival) and were beyond resuscitation. I went home on holiday during the next week. On my return to the hospital, the tragic happenings of the night of 3rd March were not discussed or hardly mentioned. No stress counselling was available then.

Activities

4. Do you think the stories in Sources E and F will appear on the proposed memorial? Give arguments for and against them being included.

5. How do they compare to the messages conveyed by the proposed memorial?

6. Construct a 'spectrum of opinion' in your classroom like the one shown below. Use sticky notes to show where you stand on the issue.

7. Discuss and justify your opinions as a class by using the Bethnal Green disaster as an example.

Memorials should show the true reality of the events they remember, even if the truth is sometimes negative. ←→ **Memorials need to focus on conveying sympathy for the victims. They are mostly concerned with remembrance, not documenting history.**

Find out more at www.stairwaytoheavenmemorial.org.

Analysing written historical representations

To analyse written representations you need to think in similar ways to when you analyse visual representations. Think about what the author has chosen to focus on, what has been included or omitted and how words are used to build an impression. Newspapers represent the past and present events in particular ways. They often have editorial sections where the people who own and control the newspaper put forward their personal opinions about the stories they include.

Source G: *The Independent,* Thursday, 19 February, 2009.

Blitz tragedy that Churchill erased from history

At the time it was hushed up. But now survivors of Britain's worst civilian tragedy, the Bethnal Green Tube shelter disaster, want a dignified memorial for its 173 victims.

Even after 65 years, remembering how Vera Trotter was killed on a winter's evening in 1943 as the Luftwaffe made one of its regular post-Blitz raids on London's East End is still enough to bring Alf Morris to tears…the 78-year-old dabs his eyes with a handkerchief as he describes the moment his father found his eight-year-old friend. 'My dad was the person who eventually identified Vera,' he recalls. 'Only the week before he'd taken a nail out of her shoe. That was the only way that he was able to recognise her.' But Vera wasn't killed by German bombs. She died in the worst civilian accident of the Second World War…a barely-reported crush of people that was kept secret for years. As the air raid warning sounded on 3 March 1943, Vera and her mother Lillian routinely gathered their bundles of bedding and made their way to Bethnal Green Tube, a brand new extension of the Central line that had yet to serve as a station but for the previous two years had become a much-needed air raid shelter with 5,000 beds.

…But Vera and Lillian never made it that night. They and 171 others were killed as they descended the eastern staircase of the station…The Bethnal Green Tube disaster, as it came to be known, was simply a tragic accident that remained buried in secrecy for decades. A small brass plaque above the entrance to Bethnal Green is the only indication for today's commuters of what happened there. But now an ever dwindling group of survivors and their descendants are hoping to build a large memorial above the steps of the Tube station to inform future generations of the tragedy. Planning permission [for the memorial] has…been approved but a lack of funds means that the £500,000 'Stairway to Heaven' seems as far away from being built as ever. Survivors like Mr. Morris are determined to have a proper memorial built before their generation dies out…'That disaster literally rocked the East End but no one wants to know about it'…Concerned that the Nazis would use the disaster for propaganda, Churchill banned media coverage… After living through the Blitz and two years of frequent bombing raids, East Enders had become more than used to the sounds of war. They would boast about being able to tell what type of bomb was falling or which anti-aircraft gun was firing from the noise it made. But no one had told locals about this particular battery of [anti-aircraft] guns that had just been installed and fired rockets instead of shells. When the guns opened up, locals assumed they were taking a direct hit and the usually orderly queues outside the Tube station descended into pandemonium. As the crush worsened, three buses drew up, disgorging even more terrified passengers into the staircase.

Activity

8. The role of the government and Churchill as prime minister are portrayed in a negative way in Source G. Complete the table to see how the newspaper has presented the situation.

Features:	Selection (what points have been chosen or left out)	Treatment (how event is presented)
Government	Didn't want people to know at the time and later on	Hushed up, barely reported
Victims		
Memorial		

How effective was Churchill's leadership during the Blitz?

In 2002 Churchill was voted 'Best Briton' in a survey carried out by the BBC. Cartoon and poster representations might help explain why so many people still view him as such a heroic figure.

Source H: A poster showing Churchill as a British bulldog in 1942.

HOLDING THE LINE !

Activity

9. Analyse how Churchill's leadership is represented in Source H. Think about his attitude and ability to unite the nation.

Analysing the views of historians

Source G presents Churchill in a different light from the common portrayals that we are used to seeing, such as Source H. Rather than contradict each other, these sources focus on different aspects of Churchill's leadership abilities and decisions.

The views of historians are also representations. Historians writing about any event have to make choices. They choose what to concentrate on and what questions they think are worth asking. They also reach views about the topics they research. Using the evidence they make judgements about the role of individuals, the reasons for an event and so on. In their writing they give their views and these sometimes differ. Their views may differ because they are looking at different things, or because they interpret the evidence differently.

Each of the historians on page 66 gives a view about how well the government provided civil defence during the Blitz, but each has a different focus.

Activity

10. Match the following descriptions to the focus of Sources I, J and K on page 66.

   a) This author is interested in the day-to-day experiences of people under the pressures of war and how this was represented at the time and after.

   b) This author provides statistical analysis of the provision of civil defence by the government.

   c) This author wants to emphasise the bravery and sense of duty in the British people.

Source I: The foreword to *Britain at War* (2002) describes the Blitz as 'a testament to the spirit of the people in what was Britain's darkest and its finest hour'. The author, Maureen Hill, explains in this extract:

> While most people were safe in shelters during an air raid or asleep in their beds on quiet nights there were large numbers of people on duty every night.

Source J: From *Warfare and the Impact of War* by John Child and Steve Waugh, 2009.

> The government gave out air raid shelters before and in the early months of the war. Some 2 million Anderson shelters were provided. These definitely saved thousands of lives by protecting people from shrapnel and flying glass. However, they offered little protection from falling masonry and many poorer people did not have gardens in which to build them. In 1941, therefore, 500,000 Morrison shelters were provided, which could be set up indoors.
>
> Only 27 per cent of people used these private shelters. The rest used public shelters or 'self-chosen' shelters, such as the London underground. At the beginning of the war, the government had rejected the use of the underground for shelter, but the force of public demand made them change their mind…
>
> Surveys suggested that only 40 per cent of Londoners regularly took shelter. This accounts for the high casualty rates. By June 1941, 43,000 civilians had been killed.

Source K: From *Britain 1914-2000* by Derrick Murphy, 2000.

> Propaganda in the press promoted a 'Britain can take it' spirit and King George VI, Queen Elizabeth and Winston Churchill visited bombed-out areas and casualties to maintain morale. But not all was bravery and defiance. Mass Observation (an agency who surveyed and published public opinions) reported shortages of bread, milk, electricity, gas and telephones. People were disoriented by shock, discomfort, disruption, dislocation, loss of sleep and confusion.

Activities

11. In what ways do the historians' accounts differ in Sources I–K?
12. Give reasons for the differences that you have identified.
13. Decide how much the differences you have found really matter.
    - Are they small differences such as a matter of detail, or big differences about the main points of the representation?
    - How much agreement is there?
    - Weigh up the similarities and differences to decide how far they differ.

Summary

- Representations are created to give an impression of an aspect of the past
- The impression is created by what is included and by the way details are drawn or by the words used
- Historians' interpretations are also representations of the past. They sometimes differ because of the historian's focus.

Evaluating representations

When you are evaluating a representation, you are deciding how good it is. When you evaluate anything in everyday life – what clothes to buy, for example – you use **criteria**. Does it fit? Is it in fashion? Is it too expensive? Is the colour right for you? You also make some criteria more important than others. If something doesn't fit, you won't buy it, even if the colour is right!

You will also use criteria when you weigh up representations of history. But let's work on an everyday example first, and then you can apply your skills to evaluating historical representations.

Using criteria to evaluate representations of history

There are many different kinds of representation. You could be judging between an extract from a history book, a cartoon, a work of historical fiction or a film portrayal of an event in the past. Apply criteria to each of them to make your judgement. But remember, in order to weigh up a historical representation you must first have good knowledge of the issue which is represented.

Using your knowledge, you can apply these tests to a representation:

- Is it **accurate**? Test the representation against what you know. Is it correct?
- Is it **complete**? Does your knowledge suggest important aspects are missing?
- Is it **objective**? Analyse the representation to see whether it is fair or unbalanced in its treatment. Here you could also think about the purpose of the author or artist.

> **Criteria:** rules or tests on which judgements can be based.

> **ResultsPlus**
> **Watch out**
>
> Never try to evaluate a representation before you have good knowledge of the issue.

Activities

1. Identify three criteria you use when you decide what to eat, then compare them with your partner. Explain whether you were influenced by any of the following factors:

   a) vegetarian beliefs

   b) dietary issues

   c) time taken.

2. With a partner pick a film or TV drama you have both seen.

   (a) Choose three criteria by which to evaluate it, for example 'funny' or 'action-packed'.

   (b) Give it a rating of 1–3 against each of the criteria, and discuss your rating with your partner. You do not need to agree, but you should each be able to back up the rating you give. Refer specifically to the film or drama.

   (c) Give the programme or film an *overall* star rating of 1–5. Make a display to explain your overall evaluation to your class, making sure you refer to the criteria you have used. Was one criterion so important that it had the most influence on your overall rating?

Cartoons as representations

Civilian reactions to the bombing were an important topic for cartoonists during the Second World War and are useful as representations for us now.

Cartoonists created many representations of the way people in Britain responded to the bombing. One common theme was the ability of the British public to keep going and not give up. British cartoonists often used rousing slogans like 'Business as usual' or 'We can take it'.

Source A: This cartoon by Joseph Lee was first published by *The Evening News* on 23 March 1940 in the 'Smiling Through' cartoon series.

Life carrying on as usual

Able and determined to overcome shortages

Adaptable and resolute

Time and enough money for family outing

Shows grit and determination

Cheerful

Encourages a sense of humour despite the difficulties

'But, George, if you're going to pull up at every inn, it's going to be as expensive as running the car.'

However, not all cartoonists took the 'Smiling Through' position. Some wanted to put pressure on the authorities to make changes to improve the ways civilians were protected during air raids.

Context for Source B

Anderson shelters were built to accommodate six people each.

People constructed them in their gardens from a government-supplied kit made from galvanised steel.

They were issued free to householders on low incomes and wealthier people paid £7.

An estimated 2 million Anderson shelters were issued throughout the war.

Most people in London did not use Anderson shelters, partly because many Londoners did not have a garden in which to put the shelter up. It is estimated that 27 per cent used Anderson shelters, 9 per cent slept in public shelters and 4 per cent used Tube stations. The rest were either working at night or stayed at home.

Activities

3. Create your own labels to analyse the representation in Source B. For example, you could use the label 'government officials' for the people hiding in the shelter.

4. What do you think is the 'Air Raid Precautions Test' that is being carried out?

5. Now discuss what you think the cartoonist is suggesting about the quality of government shelter provision.

6. Evaluate this cartoon as a representation. Draw up a chart in three columns headed: 'How accurate?', 'How Complete?' 'How Objective?' Fill in your three columns for Source B. You can use the points given in the context box, to help you add points of your own.

Source B: A cartoon by David Low, 'Air Raid Precautions Test', first published by the *London Evening Standard* on 10 February, 1939.

Evaluating representations created by historians

Historians aim to give you their view of past events. The details in their writings are likely to be accurate. But you will still need to think about whether the view they give is the best one, depending on what you want to find out. If you want a detailed view of a period in depth, then a historian looking at overviews is not the best one for you.

Look back at Activity 10 on pages 65–66. You saw that what shapes a historian's work is what the historian wants to explore and what he or she is choosing to focus on.

How did civilians in Britain react to the experience of war from 1939 to 1945?

Study Sources C and D, thinking about the historian's focus. Even if the two historians are both looking in depth or overview, they can still be looking for different things and so have a different view. You can see this in Sources C and D below. When you analyse and evaluate historians' representations, think about:

- the historian's focus
- the historian's view.

The highlighted sections should help you identify some of the key differences in how these two historians represent civilians' responses to the Blitz.

Source C: An extract from *Waiting for the All Clear*, Ben Wicks, 1990.

Fifty years ago, during the Blitz, the British people showed that they didn't have to be in uniform to be heroes. The Dunkirk spirit flowed in city streets, suburban bomb-shelters and every town and village in the land. Those at home kept their great British sense of humour in the most appalling circumstances. In hardship they looked after each other. Home Guard, firemen, policemen, air-raid wardens risked their own lives as they struggled to limit the destruction. Housewives bravely started again when their homes were lost. Out of the terror and tragedy came courage and solidarity, selflessness and an unshakable determination to win through against the awesome might of the Luftwaffe.

Source D: From *Britain 1914–2000* by Derrick Murphy, 2000.

…women and children inevitably became the victims of the Blitz because their homes were clustered around the docks and centres of industrial employment…

Over a million children were evacuated in the early stages of the war. Evacuation brought home to the public the scale of child poverty and deprivation. However, the culture clash between classes made many evacuees unhappy and they returned to their parents in 1941 as soon as the worst effects of the Blitz eased. Hitler's bombing campaigns did not bring Britain to its knees because the Luftwaffe (German air force) lacked the capacity to mount attacks over sufficiently wide areas to knock out all major industrial centres and port facilities. Moreover, despite the high rate of success achieved by German U-boats (submarines) targeting the Atlantic convoys bringing goods to Britain from the United States, sufficient supplies were delivered to keep Britain going. Domestic production of coal and arms were maintained.

ResultsPlus
Top Tip

Two students can come to different judgements about representations and still get the same marks. The important thing is to be able to show that you have used criteria and can back up your decisions using the representations themselves and your own knowledge.

Wicks and Murphy are both writing accurately, but they disagree about the relative importance of British civilians' ability to cope and carry on through the air raids. How can they have different views yet both be accurate? They can because their focus is different. One historian wants to show the bravery of civilians; the other wants to explore the problems the German forces faced in meeting their military goals.

Add another criterion to use when evaluating representations: the purpose or focus of the author.

Activities

7. Copy this chart and complete it using as many of the statements A–K as you wish. Write the statement in both columns if you think it belongs in both. Try to add some extra points of your own.

Wicks	Murphy
Notes for my overall evaluation of the representations:	

A) The author is a historian and can write from authority.

B) The author's focus is on the bravery of the British people.

C) The author's focus is on the limits of Germany's military strength.

D) The author provides information about the wider military operations of the Allies.

E) The author's focus is on the personal stories of ordinary people.

F) The author reveals the problems experienced as a result of the evacuation programme.

G) The author emphasises social unity and willingness to pull together.

H) The author blames German weaknesses for Germany's failure.

I) This representation is not exploring…

J) The author provides a positive slant on the impact of the suffering endured.

K) The author is interested in the wider political situation.

L) The author is keen to emphasise the idea that British people have special qualities of bravery and humour in adversity.

8. Which is the better representation of how British civilians reacted to the experience of war 1939–1945? Remember to evaluate both representations and give a judgement about which you think is better. Make your criteria clear. It will help if you use the vocabulary suggested on page 61.

Activity

Controlled assessment practice

9. Complete questions B (i) and (ii). Then turn to Maximise your marks on page 75 to see if you need to improve your answer.

    B (i) Study Sources C and D. They are both representations of civilian reactions to the Blitz.

    How far do these representations differ?

    B (ii) Study Sources B, C and D.

    Choose the one which you think is the best representation of how civilians responded to the experience of the Blitz. Explain your choice. You should use all three representations and your own knowledge to explain your answer.

Summary

- A historian's writing aims to be accurate and objective.
- Criteria must always be used when evaluating representations.
- The criteria could be: the accuracy, comprehensiveness, objectivity and purpose or focus of the representation.
- Representations must be evaluated in their historical context.

Results Plus
Maximise your marks

Part A Carry out a historical enquiry

In this task, you are required to carry out an enquiry; the enquiry focus will be set by Edexcel. The task is worth 20 marks and you should aim to spend about an hour writing it up. The mark scheme below shows how your work for this task will be marked.

Remember that in this task you are also assessed on the quality of your written communication: use historical terminology where appropriate, organise the information clearly and coherently, and make sure your spelling, punctuation and grammar are accurate.

Level	Responses at this level...	Marks available
Level 1	Make simple comments. There are few links between the comments and few details are given. Only one or two sources have been used in the enquiry.	1–5 marks
Level 2	Make statements about the enquiry topic. Information is included that is mostly relevant and accurate, but it is not well organised to focus on the point of the enquiry. A range of sources has been consulted and information taken from them.	6–10 marks
Level 3	Are organised to focus mainly on the point of the enquiry. Accurate and relevant information is given to support the points the student makes. A range of sources has been found and well-chosen material taken from them.	11–15 marks
Level 4	Focus well on the point of the enquiry. A well-supported conclusion is reached, for example about: the nature of change OR whether one factor was more important than the others OR the inter-relationship between two or more of the factors (depending on the enquiry focus). A range of sources appropriate to the enquiry has been identified and material from the sources has been well deployed.	16–20 marks

Let's look at an extract from one student's response to the following enquiry:

- The impact of war on women's working lives in the years 1914–1919

Student response

During the First World War, thousands of men left their jobs to join the armed forces and fight in the war. This meant that many women took over their jobs to help keep Britain going.

Before the war some women had jobs. These were especially working class women and very few married women worked at all. Also, these jobs were in very restricted areas such as domestic service and the textiles industry.

According to Nigel Kelly in his book 'War and the transformation of British society', during the First World War 'women took on jobs such as bus conductors, drivers or workers on the railways'.

Harriot Stanton Blanch in her book 'Mobilizing Woman-Power' says thousands of women worked in munitions factories, in the Land Army, in Government departments, as dock-labourers, on police patrols and in banking.

ResultsPlus
Maximise your marks

This shows that there were far more types of employment available to women during the First World War.

Ben Walsh and Christopher Culpin in 'Modern World History' explain that women were accepted into some industries more easily than others. They say that women were easily accepted into office jobs.

It was a different story in jobs which were seen as 'men's work' such as engineering. In these industries women were only employed as a last resort and only after the government started employing women in their munitions factories which set an example.

After the war many women lost their job. An article from 'The Times' in March 1919 shows that women in dockyards were being dismissed from their work when the men returned. This shows that many of the changes which happened during the war did not last.

Therefore the war did see many changes in women's work as more work was available to women and more women were employed. However, some of these changes were not permanent and women went back to their homes when the war was over.

Moderator comment

This extract indicates that the response would gain a mark in level 2.

The student describes some of the jobs which women did during the First World War and shows that many new opportunities had arisen but that not all of them lasted. The answer also correctly point out that although women did different types of work, they were more 'accepted' in some jobs than others.

The student has used a range of textbooks and an internet site to provide information. Material has been selected for relevance and the student has included notes from different sources. However, the material has not been smoothly integrated and details are taken from each source in turn. The quality of written communication is generally good, the meaning is clear and correct historical terminology is used but the information is not well organised into paragraphs, instead each point is presented separately.

To improve the response, the student should focus more centrally on the precise enquiry: the impact of the First World War on women's working lives. The student could:

- show how it took time for employment opportunities to open up to women – in fact many women lost their jobs at the start of the war

- explain how some types of work were permanently changed because of the war

- show how other things, not just types of work, but wages and working conditions, were affected by the war.

ResultsPlus
Maximise your marks

Let's look at an extract from an improved student response.

Improved student response

The First World War had a big impact on the working lives of some women. At the start of the war, women's employment actually dropped overall as Richard Van Emden and Steve Humphries explain in their book 'All Quiet on the Home Front'. This was because in 1914, women were restricted to jobs in certain areas such as domestic service and the textiles industry and many of these industries do not do well in war time. Men who volunteered for the armed forces were usually replaced by other men – many industries, especially those seen as 'male' would not consider women. According to Nigel Kelly in his book 'War and the transformation of British Society', suffragettes were so frustrated by this that they organised a protest in July 1915.

There were several reasons why women were not turned to at first. Van Emden and Humphries as well as Ben Walsh and Christopher Culpin in 'GCSE Modern World History', explain that the unions resisted the employment of women workers to begin with. Most unions did not accept women and feared that employing women would affect men's wages because women would be paid less. There were also traditional ideas about what jobs were suitable for women. For this reason many women were fairly quickly and easily accepted into offices and shops because, as Deborah Thom explains, in her article at www. tlemea.com/Thom.asp, these jobs aroused 'no social concerns' as 'office and shop work was clean, respectable and presented no obvious threat to women's health'.

By 1916 the shortage of workers had become so desperate that there was no real alternative to employing women in large numbers, even in industries which were reluctant. The government led the way by employing large numbers of women in its munitions factories. Nigel Kelly shows the wide range of employment taken on by women, including as bus conductors, drivers or railway workers. Harriot Stanton Blatch, in her book 'Mobilizing Woman-Power', which was written during the war, also explains how thousands of women worked in munitions factories, in the Land Army, in Government departments, as dock-labourers, on police patrols and in banking. Although this source is biased because the author was an activist who was campaigning for women's rights and would therefore want to show that women could do valuable work of all kinds, her examples are supported by the other evidence.

The opportunities for women in the workplace did therefore increase. Many of these new jobs were better paid, which explains why many women who worked in domestic service (which was poorly paid) left to join factories and industries which paid them better even though the working hours were long and the job difficult. However, many sources, such as 'Women on the Home Front in World War One' by Professor Joanna Bourke (www.bbc.co.uk/history/british/britain_wwone/women_employment_01.shtml) show that, generally, the war did not increase women's wages and they were still paid less than men...

Moreover, many of these opportunities did not last after the war. Many women lost their jobs. An article from 'The Times' in March 1919 shows that women in dockyards were being dismissed from their work when the men returned. This is one example of how women who were employed in 'men's jobs' were only accepted during the war itself. In other industries, particularly the civil service, banking and other office jobs, women were more likely to keep their war-time job.

ResultsPlus
Maximise your marks

Part B(i) Compare two representations

In this task, you are required to analyse and compare two representations of history. The task is worth 10 marks and you should aim to spend about 30 minutes writing it up. The mark scheme below shows how your work for this task will be marked.

Level	Answers at this level...	Marks available
Level 1	Identify the main features of the two representations by giving descriptions, direct quotations, or paraphrases from one or both representations.	1–3 marks
Level 2	Identify the differences in two representations by comparing similarities and/or differences in their details.	4–7 marks
Level 3	Show understanding of the similarities and/or differences in the way the past is represented in the two extracts. The answer uses precisely selected detail from the two representations to support the explanations and the judgement about how far the representations differ.	8–10 marks

Let's look at an extract from one student's response to the representations below.

- Study Sources C and D on page 70. They are both representations of how British civilians responded to the Blitz. How far do these representations differ? (10 marks)

Student response

Sources C and D are both about British civilians. Wicks says that the British were brave and kept their sense of humour. He says they took care of each other to help them through the problems. Source C tells us about the different organisations that were set up to give assistance, like the air raid wardens. Murphy in Source D agrees that the British people faced terrible problems. However, he talks more about how difficult it was for children to live with strangers. He also talks about the Germans, but Wicks doesn't. He says the German air force lacked the capacity to mount attacks over sufficiently wide areas. So overall they differ quite a bit, because Source C talks about the British heroes and Source D talks about the German tactics.

Results Plus
Maximise your marks

Moderator comment

In this part of the answer, the student has comprehended the details in the representations and is comparing them. We can see the language of comparison is used: 'both about', 'more about', 'doesn't [talk about]', agrees, 'differ quite a bit'.

The student has noted the details which are similar in both sources and also where one author provides details which the other has not included. The student has also noted that there is a disagreement about how well British civilians coped during the Blitz.

There is enough comprehension and comparison for the answer to get into level 2, but the answer concentrates mainly on differences in details in the two sources. To raise the response to the next level, the answer should show more awareness of the differences in the portrayal of reactions to the Blitz in these two representations. Source C's focus is on how civilians pulled together and Wicks portrays unity as the most important feature of explaining how people managed. Source D's focus is on German military strategy and how the shortcomings meant British civilians could keep going. The student notes that the 'German air force lacked the capacity to mount attacks over sufficiently wide areas' but has only taken these words from the source. This aspect of the response should be much more developed.

Lets look at an improved version of this answer.

Improved student response

Sources C and D are both about British reactions to the Blitz and the extent to which they were able to cope. Murphy and Wicks consider the impact of civilian bombing and how the lives of ordinary people were affected. Source C focuses on the idea of the British character being resilient, for example by explaining how women rebuilt their homes and lives after being bombed out. Murphy also looks at the impact on family life by considering how evacuated children and their host families were affected. In contrast to Wicks, he emphasises in Source D that young people found it hard to be forced to live with people who came from such different social backgrounds.

The big difference between Sources C and D is what they are focusing on. Wicks is concerned to portray Britain as united and points to the idea that the British character showed real determination and bravery. He backs this up by giving examples of how different people from different walks of life did their bit, including older people in the Home Guard and people in the emergency services like firemen. Murphy, on the other hand is looking at the problems that were faced and shows that Britain wasn't so united, at least when you consider the reactions of people thrown together by the evacuation programme. Murphy also focuses on the tactics of the German military attacks. He claims that the Luftwaffe was simply unable to carry out raids that were extensive enough to wipe out enough British city and port areas. As a result the British people were able to keep going. So the sources agree that the British public had to face terrible difficulties but their portrayals are different. Source C gives the impression that Blitz spirit was the deciding factor in Britain holding out, whereas Source D, although not dismissing the importance of the hardships faced, puts it down to a lack of German resources. Wicks manages to put a positive slant on the suffering that was endured, whereas Murphy describes the civilians as 'victims of the Blitz'.

Part B(ii) Analyse and evaluate three representations

In this task, you are required to analyse and evaluate three representations of history. The task is worth 20 marks and you should aim to spend about an hour writing it up. The mark scheme below shows how your work for this task will be marked. Remember that in this task you are also assessed on the quality of your written communication: use historical terminology where appropriate, organise the information clearly and coherently, and make sure your spelling, punctuation and grammar are accurate.

Level	Answers at this level...	Marks available
Level 1	Show some understanding of the main features of the sources and select material. Simple judgements are made about the representation, and a limited amount of accurate information about the period is given. The material is not detailed; links between the information and the representation are not explicit.	1–5 marks
Level 2	Show an understanding of the main features of the three sources and select key features of the representations from them. Judgement is made about the best representation and detailed and accurate information about the period is added. There is little linkage between description and judgement. Judgements may relate to the accuracy or comprehensiveness of the representation.	6–10 marks
Level 3	Analyse the three sources and show some of the ways in which the past situation has been represented. Detail from the sources is used to support the analysis. There is a critical evaluation of each representation based on well selected information about the period and at least two clear criteria are applied, for example, the author's purpose or objectivity, or the accuracy, comprehensiveness of the representation.	11–15 marks
Level 4	Analyse the three sources to show the way in which the past situation has been represented. Precisely selected detail from the sources is used to support the analysis. There is a critical evaluation of the representation based on precisely selected information about the period and applying at least three criteria, for example the author's purposes or objectivity, or the comprehensiveness and/or accuracy of the representation.	16–20 marks

Let's look at an extract from one student's response.

- B(ii) Study Sources C and D from page 70 again and also Source B from page 69. Choose the one which you think is the best representation of how British civilians responded to the experience of the Blitz. You should use all three representations and your own knowledge to explain your answer. (20 marks)

Student response

I think Source B is useful because it shows that the public tried to have a sense of humour about the problems they faced. But it's not very complete because it's more about some people criticising the government for not giving them good enough shelters. We don't know if everyone was unhappy with their shelters.

I think Source C is useful because it tells us about the different organisations that were set up to help people in the Blitz. It tells us about how people pulled together to get through the hardships. But it doesn't tell us much about the people who found it more difficult to keep going. It makes it sound very positive.

I think Source D is the best. It gives us accurate information about the problems during the Blitz as well as the ways that people tried to help each other. It gives us details about the evacuation programme and why a lot of children were unhappy. It also tells us about how the Germans stopped goods getting to Britain, not just about the air raids. It is more comprehensive than the other two representations.

Moderator comment

The student has made a short comment which identifies the information which each representation can provide. The comment that Source B is not complete should be further developed to consider what we can learn about how the authorities made provision for public shelters.

The student has begun to use some criteria to evaluate the representations, but none of the comments is developed very far. The student uses the criterion of completeness to evaluate Source B. This is a good choice of a criterion by which to evaluate a cartoon. But the student uses only a limited amount of own knowledge to test this idea and does not develop the point about which parts of Source B make it 'not very complete'. To improve the answer, the student should make more use of contextual knowledge and analyse the cartoon more fully to show its limitations.

In evaluating Sources C and D, the student has chosen a valid criterion for the best representation of the responses to the Blitz – what the sources tell us about how well people coped. Here the student is basing the judgement on the focus of the representations, though this should be made more explicit. However the student's comments need to make much more use of contextual knowledge – particularly in relation to German military tactics, since the student uses this criterion to evaluate Source C as 'not comprehensive' and Source D as 'best'.

To reach the highest level the student must also make use of more criteria – three should be used to rate each representation.

Let's look at an extract from an improved student response.

Extract from student's improved answer

Source B portrays the British public as angry and resentful about the government provision of Anderson shelters. The cartoonist makes the point that the authorities are hiding from the public as they don't want to face the criticism. The crowds behind the fence are hurling stones at the shelter and the caption is mocking by saying that it is a 'test' of the strength of the shelter. The representation shows that some people were frightened during the raids and we know that some people pressurised the authorities to allow them to use the tube stations as shelters as they felt safer underground. We don't know how widespread this anger was felt and therefore the representation is not comprehensive. It is not objective because, as it is a London newspaper, it focuses on the views of its London readers rather than the wider population across Britain. We know that many people preferred to stay in their own homes during the raids but we don't know whether this was due to them being too scared to stay in the Anderson shelters because they felt insecure as represented in the cartoon.

This links to Source C, which, in contrast, portrays the British public as heroic and resourceful rather than resentful. Wicks claims that the spirit of Dunkirk was present throughout Britain too, but we know that the events at Dunkirk were deliberately presented to the British public as a triumph whereas it was very nearly a disaster for the British armed forces. Wicks argues that the British were 'unshakeable' in their determination and bravery to carry on as usual and win the war. However, many reports from the time suggest that the government was very worried to keep up morale and that is why details about events like Dunkirk were heavily censored and subject to propaganda. Wicks wants the reader to focus on the idea that British people are particularly brave and heroic and stood up to the 'awesome' Luftwaffe.

Source D appears to be the best of the three representations for the following reasons. Firstly, it is more comprehensive. It is concerned with the wider political and economic history of the Blitz rather than concentrating on personal stories of heroism… It is also more balanced. It looks at the situation from the point of view of German military tactics and capabilities rather than simply looking at the experiences of British civilians on the ground. Murphy also takes a more objective stand when looking at the economic and social problems that the war showed up in British society rather than a more romantic picture presented by Wicks whose focus is more about patriotism.

Glossary

Auxiliary armed services: these are military services which support the fighting forces but are not directly involved in fighting.

Blitz: the sustained bombing of Britain by Nazi Germany, 1940–41.

Capitulation: the act of surrendering or giving up.

Censorship: the control by a government of the spread of all information that might be useful to the enemy or that might upset the morale of the public.

Communiqués: official reports often sent in a hurry.

Criteria: rules or tests on which judgements can be based.

Dunkirk: in May 1940, after the Germans had invaded France, defeated British and French soldiers fled to the port of Dunkirk in Northern France where many were rescued by boat and brought back to Britain.

Economic depression: when trade drops, businesses fail and unemployment is increased.

Evacuation: the process of moving people from towns and cities into the countryside for safety, to protect them from German bombing.

Flappers: young women of the 1920s who challenged traditional ideas through fashion and social habits.

Gas masks: everyone in Britain was given a gas mask which allowed them to breathe if gas bombs were dropped – but no attacks took place.

Intern: to force someone to live in a special area or camp.

Inter-war: between the two world wars.

Land Army: a British civilian force during the First and Second World Wars made up of women who worked in farming and replaced men who had gone to fight. These women were commonly known as 'Land Girls'.

Military conscription: the system of forcing men and sometimes women to serve in the armed forces.

Phoney War: the period from September 1939 to April 1940 when little fighting took place and there were no enemy bombing raids.

Propaganda: one-sided information used to persuade people to support certain ideas or beliefs.

Rationing: the setting of a fixed allowance of food and other provisions for each person to prevent shortages.

Total war: war fought with all available resources, intended to destroy entirely all enemy resistance and affecting civilians as well as soldiers.

Traumatised: psychologically deeply upset as a result of a bad experience – in this case the bombing raids.

Published by Pearson Education Limited, a company incorporated in England and Wales, having its registered office at Edinburgh Gate, Harlow, Essex, CM20 2JE. Registered company number: 872828

Edexcel is a registered trademark of Edexcel Limited

Text © Pearson Education Limited

The rights of Steve Waugh, Victoria Payne and Kirsty Taylor have been asserted by them in accordance with the Copyright, Designs and Patents Act 1988.

First published 2010

12 11 10
10 9 8 7 6 5 4 3 2 1

British Library Cataloguing in Publication Data
A catalogue record for this book is available from the British Library.

ISBN 978 1 846908 79 8

Designed and typeset by Juice Creative Ltd, Hertfordshire
Original illustrations © Pearson Education Ltd 2010
Printed in Great Britain at Scotprint, Haddington

Picture credits
The publisher would like to thank the following for their kind permission to reproduce their photographs:

(Key: b-bottom; c-centre; l-left; r-right; t-top)

Alamy Images: Trevor Smithers ARPS 33, Peter Marshall 21, Trinity Mirror / Mirrorpix 57; **Corbis:** 58, Hulton-Deutsch Collection 14, 37, Hulton-Deutsch Collection 14, 37, Stapleton Collection 12, David Pollack 5; **Mary Evans Picture Library:** Illustrated London News Ltd 19, Robert Hunt Collection / Imperial War Museum 25; **Getty Images:** 17, Galerie Bilderwelt 65, Fred Morley 55, Fox Photos 54, Popperfoto 28; **Image courtesy of The Advertising Archives:** 38; **Imperial War Museum:** 13, Bert P.S. Thomas 30; **Angela Leonard:** 61; **Bradford Museum and Libraries:** 34; **Arboreal Architecture Ltd:** 63; **Vinmag Archive Ltd:** 9; **Photolibrary.com:** Rod Edwards / Britain on View 60; **Rex Features:** Nicholas Bailey 62; **Solo Syndication / Associated Newspapers Ltd:** David Low / Evening Standard / British Cartoon Archive, University of Kent 69, Joseph Lee / Evening News / British Cartoon Archive, University of Kent 68; **TopFoto:** 10

Cover images: *Front: ***Getty Images:** Fox Photos / Hulton Archive

All other images © Pearson Education

Every effort has been made to trace the copyright holders and we apologise in advance for any unintentional omissions. We would be pleased to insert the appropriate acknowledgement in any subsequent edition of this publication.

We are grateful to the following for permission to reproduce copyright material:

Tables
Table on page 27 from *Bombers & Mash: The Domestic Front, 1939-45*, Virago (Raynes Minns, 1999) reproduced by permission of Little, Brown Book Group Limited and Johnson & Alcock Ltd; Table on page 37 from *Britain in the Age of Total War*, Heinemann (M. Chandler, 2002) p.21, copyright © Pearson Education Limited; Table on page 48 from *Edexcel GCSE Modern World History Unit 3A War and the Transformation of British Society C.1903-28 Student Book*, Edexcel, Modern World History Texts (Nigel Kelly 2009) p.56, copyright © Edexcel Limited.

Text
Extract on page 20 quoted and adapted from the words of Captain H.M. Myers, originally published in the commemorative book "Home Guarding" (1945) and since 2005 online in the Staffordshire Home Guard website www.staffshomeguard.co.uk, granted with kind permission of the Myers family; Extract on page 46 from *Edexcel GCSE Modern World History*, Third edition, Hodder Educaton (Ben Walsh and Christopher Culpin 2010) p.324, copyright © Hodder Education; Extract on page 48 from *Edexcel GCSE Modern World History Unit 3A War and the Transformation of British Society C.1903-28 Student Book*, Edexcel, Modern World History Texts (Nigel Kelly 2009) pp.54,56, copyright © Edexcel Limited; Extract on page 49 after "Women on the Home Front in World War One", BBC, 05/11/2009 (by Professor Joanna Bourke), www.bbc.co.uk/history, copyright © The BBC; Extract on page 49 from "Women in Dockyards, More Dismissals", The Times, 01/03/1919, copyright © *The Times* 1919, www.nisyndication.com; Extract on page 51 from *Edexcel GCSE Modern World History*, Third Edition, Hodder Education (Ben Walsh and Christopher Culpin 2010) p.369, copyright © Hodder Education; Quote on page 51 from Sir Winston Churchill at Lord Mayor's Lunch in London, 09/11/1943, Reproduced with permission of Curtis Brown Ltd, London on behalf of the Estate of Sir Winston Churchill, copyright © Winston S. Churchill; Extract on page 51 from "National Health Service History" by Geoffrey Rivett, http://www.nhshistory.net/intro1.htm, reproduced with permission; Extract on page 51 from 'What Britain thinks of The Beveridge Report' as shown by a Gallup Poll by the British Institute of Public Opinion in 1942-3 Catalogue ref: PREM 4/89/2, http://www.nationalarchives.gov.uk/pathways/citizenship/brave_new_world/docs/beveridge_public.htm, by kind permission of the Gallup Organisation; Extract on page 63 by Doris Russell, www.stairwaytoheavenmemorial.org, copyright © Stairway to Heaven Memorial Trust 2007. All Rights Reserved; Extract on page 64 after "The Blitz tragedy that Churchill erased from history", *The Independent*, 19/02/2009 (Taylor, J.), copyright © The Independent.

In some instances we have been unable to trace the owners or clarify the full rights of copyright material, and we would appreciate any information that would enable us to do so.

Websites
The websites used in this book were correct and up to date at the time of publication. It is essential for tutors to preview each website before using it in class so as to ensure that the URL is still accurate, relevant and appropriate. We suggest that tutors bookmark useful websites and consider enabling students to access them through the school/college intranet.

Disclaimer
This material has been published on behalf of Edexcel and offers high-quality support for the delivery of Edexcel qualifications. This does not mean that the material is essential to achieve any Edexcel qualification, nor does it mean that it is the only suitable material available to support any Edexcel qualification. Edexcel material will not be used verbatim in setting any Edexcel examination or assessment. Any resource lists produced by Edexcel shall include this and other appropriate resources.

Copies of official specifications for all Edexcel qualifications may be found on the Edexcel website: www.edexcel.com